Faith WEALTH & FIRDAWS

بِسْمِ ٱللَّهِ ٱلرَّحْمَٰنِ ٱلرَّحِيمِ

FAITH, WEALTH AND FIRDAWS

The PURE Framework for Building a Life of Faith, Wealth and Legacy

---

By

Folu Umm Abdullah

Firdaws Press

ISBN 979-8-90417-889-5

Published by Firdaws Press
London, United Kingdom

Cover design by Folu Umm Abdullah

Interior design by Folu Umm Abdullah

Second Edition: 2026

May the insights, reflections, and guidance in these pages be a source of blessing, clarity and growth in your journey to Al-Firdaws.

DEDICATION

To the Muslim sister who knows she was created for more.

More sincerity in her worship.

More intention in how she lives.

More courage in how she builds.

To the sister whose heart longs to draw nearer to Allah ﷻ while still striving to grow, contribute and create impact in this world.

To the sister who carries responsibility with quiet strength, for her family, her community and the legacy she hopes to leave behind.

This book is for the one who refuses to believe that faith and ambition must exist in opposition.

For the one who believes she can pursue excellence, build wealth with integrity, lead with character and still keep her heart firmly anchored to Allah ﷻ.

May Allah ﷻ guide your steps with clarity, anchor your heart in sincerity and place barakah in everything you build.

"And that there is not for man except that [good] for which he strives" (Surah An-Najm 53:39)

TABLE OF CONTENTS

ACKNOWLEDGEMENTS

I begin with gratitude to Allah ﷻ, the Most High.

Alhamdulillah for every breath, every moment of clarity and every opportunity He granted that made this work possible. Without His guidance, mercy and permission, none of these words would have found their way onto these pages.

To the sisters whose experiences, reflections and quiet strength inspired so much of what is written here, your sincerity, resilience and determination are woven throughout this book. Your journeys continue to remind me that growth, leadership and contribution are most powerful when they remain anchored in faith.

To my loved ones who supported this work with patience, encouragement and heartfelt dua, your presence and belief made this journey lighter than it might otherwise have been. You are present in these pages in ways that words cannot fully capture.

To my teachers, mentors and the scholars whose knowledge and example shaped my understanding, your guidance continues to illuminate my path. May Allah ﷻ reward you for every insight shared, every lesson taught and every intention that helped bring this work into being.

And to you, dear reader, thank you for choosing reflection, growth and a life directed toward Allah ﷻ.

May this book become a companion on your journey, helping you build a life of faith, responsibility, contribution and lasting legacy, while keeping your heart firmly oriented toward the gardens of Al-Firdaws.

I pray that Allah ﷻ accepts our intentions, blesses our efforts and grants us all the honour of entering Jannatul Firdaws.

Ameen.

LETTER FROM FOLU UMM ABDULLAH

In the name of Allah, the Most Gracious, the Most Merciful.

The One who guides hearts when they waver, expands paths when they feel narrow and never abandons those who return to Him.

May He bless our efforts with what is pure and halal, place sincerity in our intentions and allow every step we take to bring us closer to Him.

My dear sister,

As-salamu alaikum wa rahmatullahi wa barakatuh.

Over the years, I have had the privilege of walking alongside many remarkable Muslim women, women who are educated, capable and committed to striving to live in a way that pleases Allah ﷻ. Women who are building, contributing and carrying responsibility across their work, families and communities.

From the outside, they appear strong and accomplished, yet behind that strength, I often hear quiet questions that are rarely spoken aloud:

Am I doing enough for my akhirah while striving in this world?

Why does balance feel so difficult, even when my intentions are sincere?

Is it possible to grow, build and lead without losing sight of what truly matters?

These questions are not unfamiliar to me. I have known the weight of responsibility, the desire to excel, to contribute and to honour what has been entrusted to me.

I have also known moments of quiet exhaustion when the heart wonders whether it is possible to build a meaningful life without becoming fragmented along the way.

Through these reflections, one thing became clear:

Many of us are not lacking ambition, discipline or faith.

What we often lack is structure. A way of living that allows our faith, our growth and our responsibilities to exist in alignment.

From this, **The PURE Framework** was developed.

A structure built on **four disciplines and sixteen guiding principles** designed to guide how a Muslim woman lives, builds and grows.

Purpose — living and building a life with clarity and responsibility

Unity — strengthening the relationships that sustain you

Reputation — developing influence through integrity and character

Emaan — nurturing the spiritual depth that anchors everything

Together, they form a way of building a life that grows in both dunya and akhirah. A life where faith remains the foundation even as responsibility increases, where wealth is pursued with intention and understood as an amanah, where leadership is exercised with sincerity and where what is built carries forward.

This book is my offering to you.

A guide to the **PURE Framework and its sixteen principles,** a companion for reflection and alignment, a reminder that success is not only measured by what you achieve, but by how you build, who you uplift and what remains.

My prayer is that within these pages, you find clarity where there was uncertainty, intention where there was distraction and direction in how you move forward.

May this journey bring you closer to Allah ﷻ and may what you build in this life lead you to the gardens of Al-Firdaws in the next.

With love and dua,

Folu Umm Abdullah

Founder, The Firdaws Connection.

INTRODUCTION TO THE PURE FRAMEWORK

Four Disciplines. Sixteen Principles. One Pathway

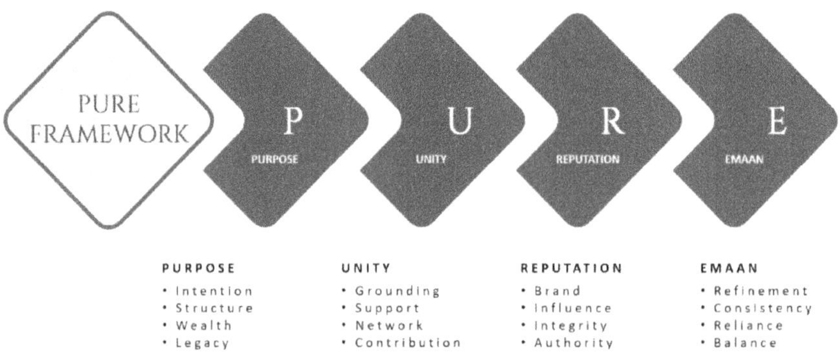

Many sisters strive to improve their lives, yet often feel pulled in different directions. They seek success in their careers while longing for a deeper spiritual connection. They wish to contribute to their families and communities while still finding time to nurture their own growth. They aspire to build stability, influence and meaningful work without losing sight of what truly matters.

For many Muslim women, the challenge is not a lack of ambition, discipline or faith. It is the absence of a structure that allows these elements to grow together.

The **PURE Framework** was developed to provide that structure.

The PURE Framework is a faith-centred model designed to help Muslim women cultivate lives that are spiritually grounded, intellectually purposeful and aligned with their ultimate return to Allah ﷻ.

The framework is built upon **four disciplines and sixteen guiding principles,** each representing an essential dimension of a balanced and intentional life.

Each discipline strengthens the others, creating balance between faith, growth and impact.

Together, they offer a pathway for building a life that honours both **dunya and akhirah.**

PURE does not address one area of your life while neglecting the others. It recognises that a woman's life moves as an integrated whole;

Her worship shapes her work.

Her relationships shape her wellbeing.

Her wealth shapes her capacity to contribute.

Her spiritual grounding shapes every decision she makes.

When these dimensions are nurtured together, even gradually, success moves beyond isolated achievement.

It becomes a way of life

A life where faith remains central as responsibility grows. Where ambition and worship strengthen rather than compete with one another and where what is built in one area naturally supports what is being built in another.

The Four Disciplines of the PURE Framework

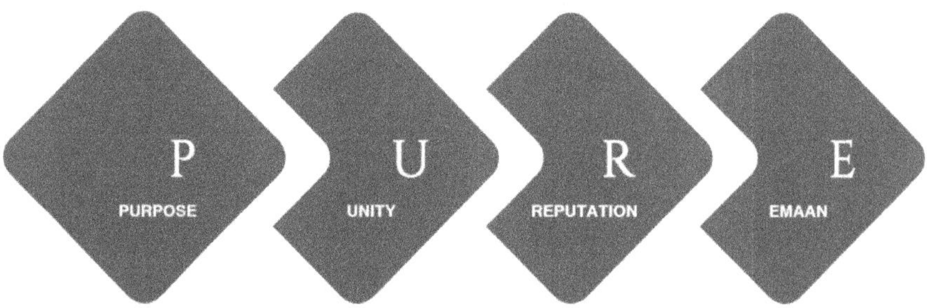

Purpose

Living and Building With Intention

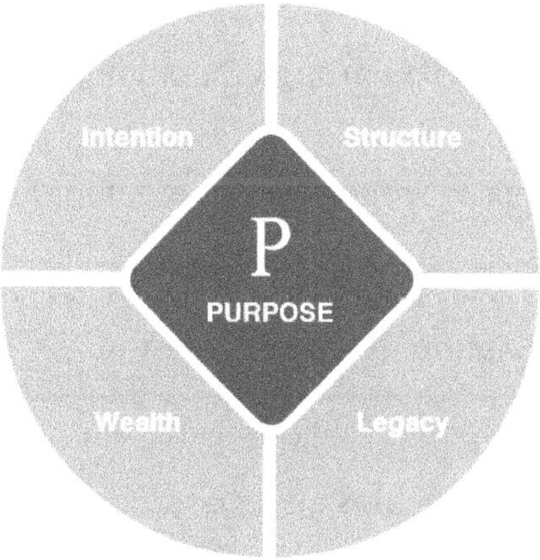

Purpose is the discipline that directs how you live, build and make decisions. It ensures that the life you pursue reflects both your values and your responsibility before Allah ﷻ.

Through the principles of:

Intention — Acting with sincerity so success never comes at the cost of the soul.

Structure — Designing a life that supports spiritual, personal and professional growth.

Wealth — Viewing wealth as an amanah to be built responsibly and used wisely.

Legacy — Making decisions that continue to benefit others long after you are gone.

Purpose ensures that what you build today contributes to

something that endures.

Unity

Strength Through Belonging

Unity recognises that meaningful growth is rarely achieved in isolation. It is strengthened through grounding, relationships and shared advancement.

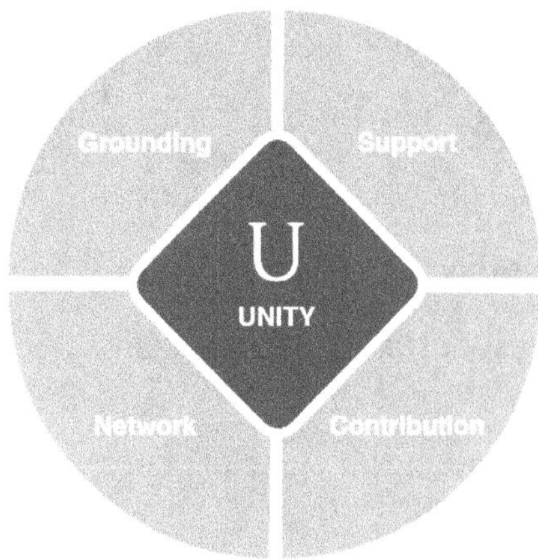

Through the principles of:

Grounding — Understanding who you are through the lens of faith.

Support — Creating environments and relationships that sustain growth.

Network — Building intentional connections that expand opportunity and strengthen the Ummah.

Contribution — Using your abilities to uplift others and serve something greater than yourself.

Unity reminds us that the strongest lives are built not alone, but within community.

Reputation

Influence Built With Integrity

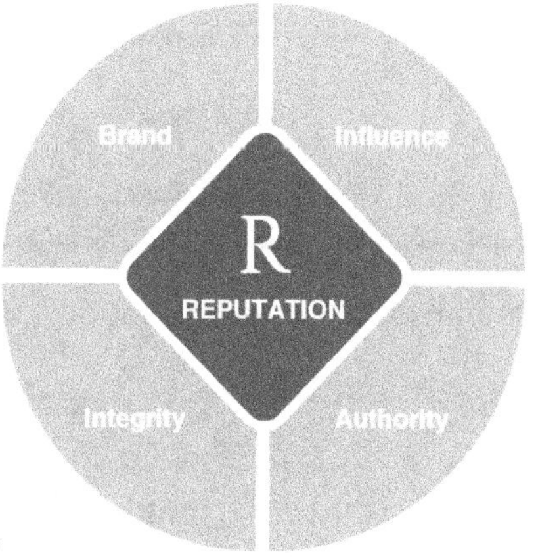

As someone takes on more responsibilities and becomes more visible, their influence naturally increases.

Reputation is the discipline that ensures this influence is guided by integrity, character and sincerity.

Through the principles of:

Brand — Presenting an identity that reflects faith, values and authenticity.

Influence — Using your voice and presence to guide, inspire and uplift others.

Integrity — Ensuring that your actions remain aligned with your values.

Authority — Building credibility and trust through consistent character and excellence.

Reputation shapes how a person is trusted, remembered and followed.

Emaan

Spiritual Depth That Anchors Everything

Emaan is the inner foundation that protects the heart as life expands outwardly.

Without spiritual grounding, success can become hollow, and achievement can lose its meaning.

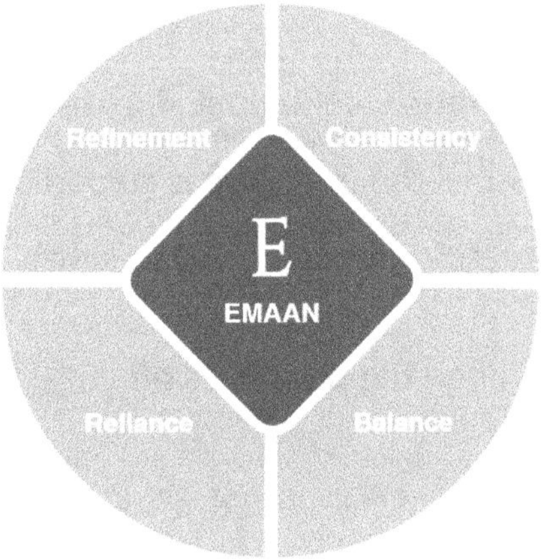

Through the principles of:

Refinement — Continually purifying the heart, intentions and actions.

Consistency — Honouring the small deeds that sustain spiritual strength.

Reliance — Working with excellence while trusting Allah with outcomes.

Balance — Pursuing dunya without neglecting the akhirah.

Emaan safeguards the believer so that growth never distances them from the One who grants it.

Living the Framework

The PURE Framework is a system for living.

Its disciplines and principles work together to support a life that grows in multiple dimensions at once:

Spiritual depth.

Personal clarity.

Meaningful relationships.

Responsible influence.

Lasting legacy.

When these elements are nurtured together, success goes beyond worldly achievement, it becomes a life built with purpose, lived with sincerity and aimed toward the ultimate goal, **Al-Firdaws.**

HOW TO USE THIS BOOK

Faith, Wealth, and Firdaws is created for you to experience, reflect on, and revisit as your life changes.

The Structure of This Book

The author organized this book according to **the four disciplines of The PURE Framework.**

Each section starts with a **PURE Introduction.** It explains the discipline and how it helps shape a balanced, intentional life.

In each section, you'll explore **four disciplines**. Together, they create the sixteen principles that form the complete framework.

Each chapter highlights one principle. It follows a clear structure that takes you from reflection to action.

What You Will Find in Each Chapter

The Principle

Each chapter introduces one of the sixteen principles of the PURE Framework. It explains what the principle means and how it helps shape a life of faith, leadership, and purpose.

The Pure Connection

A short persona story that illustrates the principle to life through a relatable experience. These stories show how the framework's principles show up in daily life and how they can guide decisions, priorities and growth.

Firdaws Reflection

A series of thoughtful prompts designed to encourage honest self-reflection. These questions invite you to pause and notice the habits, patterns or views that shape your life now.

Wisdom Unfolded

A brief reflection connecting the chapter's message with the Qur'an and Sunnah. They offer timeless wisdom for personal growth. By following these teachings, we can nurture our development in line with Islamic values.

Principle in Action

Practical exercises that help translate reflection into meaningful action. These steps are designed to support gradual, sustainable growth rather than overwhelming transformation.

A Dua to Carry With You

Authentic supplications drawn from trusted sources, reminding us that all change ultimately comes from the mercy of Allah ﷻ.

PURE Practice

One simple micro-practice you can begin immediately.

Small, consistent actions often create the most meaningful transformation over time. These practices are designed to help you apply the principle practically and sustainably.

How to Approach This Book

Read it with care and reflect thoroughly. Allow yourself the space to pause, journal and revisit chapters when needed. Growth rarely happens through urgency. It unfolds through awareness, intention and consistent effort.

You can read the book sequentially and return to specific principles depending on the stage of life you find yourself in.

The goal is **alignment.**

> Alignment between faith and ambition.
>
> Alignment between effort and reliance upon Allah ﷻ.
>
> Alignment between the life you build and the legacy you leave behind.

PART ONE

PURPOSE

Living and Building With Intention

إِنَّ ٱلَّذِينَ ءَامَنُوا۟ وَعَمِلُوا۟ ٱلصَّـٰلِحَـٰتِ كَانَتْ لَهُمْ جَنَّـٰتُ
ٱلْفِرْدَوْسِ نُزُلًا ١٠٧

'Indeed, those who have believed and done righteous deeds – they will have the Gardens of Paradise as a lodging,'

Surah Al-Kahf 18:107

A life lived with honest intention and righteous action moves steadily toward

PURE INTRODUCTION

PURPOSE

Living and Building With Intention

Every life is shaped, through choices made daily, through priorities set, consciously or unconsciously, through the direction a person allows themselves to follow, yet many people move through life without ever stopping to ask a defining question:

Am I living with intention, or simply responding to what is in front of me?

A life without purpose does not necessarily look empty.

It can still appear productive, full and even successful, but beneath all that busyness, there's often no clear direction. People put in effort, but it doesn't always focus on what truly matters.

Purpose brings clarity.

It allows a woman to understand not only what she is doing, but why she is doing it.

For a Muslim woman, purpose is not self-defined alone, it is anchored in her relationship with Allah ﷻ.

It shapes how she earns, how she builds, how she spends and how she gives. It influences the way she approaches her responsibilities, her ambitions and her long-term vision.

Without purpose, effort can become scattered.

With purpose, effort becomes directed.

Purpose extends beyond work and wealth alone; it shapes how a Muslimah cares for her body, how she rests and how she sustains the energy required for everything else she carries.

Within the PURE Framework, Purpose is expressed through four principles:

Intention — Acting with sincerity so success never comes at the cost of the soul

Structure — Designing a life that fosters growth in spiritual, professional, and financial aspects.

Wealth — Viewing wealth as an amanah to be built responsibly and used wisely

Legacy — Making decisions today that continue to benefit others long after you are gone

Together, these principles ensure that what is built is both successful and meaningful.

Because a life of faith, wealth and legacy is not built by accident, it is built with intention.

CHAPTER ONE

Intention: Acting With Sincerity So Success Never Comes At The Cost Of The Soul

Principle Introduction

Every action begins with an intention.

Whether spoken or unspoken, clear or unnoticed, intention shapes the direction and meaning of what we do.

It determines not only the outcome of an action, but its value.

A person may pursue success, build wealth and achieve recognition. But without intention, these pursuits can become disconnected from what truly matters.

They may bring results.

But not always fulfilment.

For a Muslim woman, intention is what anchors action in faith.

It transforms everyday efforts into acts of worship. It ensures that success is not pursued at the expense of the soul, but in alignment with it.

Without intention, it is easy to drift.

To follow opportunities without reflection.

To make decisions based on urgency rather than clarity.

To pursue outcomes without considering their impact.

With intention, everything becomes more deliberate.

Choices become clearer.

Actions become more meaningful.

And growth becomes aligned with purpose.

The Pure Connection

The Seeker

Rashida had always driven herself.

She focused on her goals, worked hard, and took pride in achieving what she aimed for.

Over time, her efforts brought results. She progressed in her career. She gained recognition for her work. She built a life that reflected discipline and ambition. From the outside, everything appeared successful. But internally, there were moments she struggled to define.

Moments when, despite all she had built, she felt a quiet disconnection.

Not constant, but it was noticeable.

One evening, after a tough week, she sat quietly for the first time in a while.

No deadlines.

No immediate responsibilities.

Just space.

And within that space, a question surfaced:

Why am I doing all of this?

The question unsettled her. It wasn't that she lacked an answer. It was that she had never taken the time to define it.

She was moving with momentum. She responded to opportunities, met expectations, and kept going. But she had not consciously anchored her actions in intention.

In the days that followed, she began to reflect more deeply. She revisited her goals; she needed to understand them. She asked herself what she wanted her efforts to represent.

What kind of life she was building.

Who she wanted to become through what she was doing.

That shift did not change her external life immediately, but it changed how she approached it.

Her actions became more intentional. Her decisions are more considered. Her sense of direction is more grounded. She was no longer moving without clarity, she was moving with intention.

Firdaws Reflection

Intention begins with awareness.

Take a moment to reflect:

- What currently drives your decisions and actions?
- Are your goals aligned with your values?
- How often do you pause to set intention before acting?
- Are there areas of your life where you feel you are moving without clarity?

A life of intention begins when you pause long enough to ask why.

Wisdom Unfolded

The Prophet ﷺ taught us:

“Actions are judged by intentions, and every person will have what they intended.”

(Bukhari & Muslim)

This hadith establishes a foundational truth.

It reminds us that the value of an action is not only in what is done, but in the intention behind it.

Two people may pursue the same goal.

But their outcomes, in both this life and the next, may differ completely based on what resides in their hearts.

Principle in Action

Clarifying Your Intentions

Living with intention requires conscious reflection.

Use the following exercise to bring clarity to your actions.

Alignment requires a moment of pause.

Use the following exercise to explore the intentions currently shaping your life.

Step One: Reconnect With Your Deeper Purpose

Identify 1-3 values you want your life to consistently express.

Examples:

- Faith & spiritual growth
- Family & connection
- Professional excellence
- Health & energy
- Learning & growth
- Compassion & service

Prompt: If my actions naturally reflected these values, what would that look like?

Step Two: Identify Your Current Direction

Take a moment to consider the areas where you invest most of your time and energy.

Reflect on the following questions:

- What responsibilities currently occupy the majority of my time?
- What goals am I actively pursuing at this stage of my life?
- Which choices match my values? Which ones feel driven by outside expectations?

Awareness is the first step toward intentional change

Step Three: Define a *short, meaningful intention* for this season of life.

Examples:

- "To lead with clarity and calm."
- "To nurture my family while honouring my professional growth."
- "To invest in my hereafter through sadaqah jariyah."

Reminder: This is not a goal; it is a compass to guide choices and energy.

Step Four: Align One Area of Your Life

Rather than attempting to transform everything at once, focus on one area of your life.

This could be:

- your work
- your family responsibilities
- your personal development
- your service to others

Ask yourself:
How can I consciously align this area of my life with a sincere intention to seek the pleasure of Allah?

Small changes in intention can lead to big shifts in how we feel about our daily tasks.

When intention becomes clear, effort gains meaning.

And when effort is aligned with sincere intention, even the ordinary routines of life begin to carry spiritual value.

A Dua to Carry With You

Dua for sincerity

اللهم اجعل عملي كله صالحا واجعله لوجهك خالصا ولا تجعل لاحد فيه شيئا

Transliteration:

Allāhumma aj'l 'amalī kullahu ṣālḥā wāj'lh Liwajhika khālṣā wa-lā tj'l li-aḥad fīhi shay'an

Translation:

O Allah ﷻ, make all my deeds righteous and make them sincerely for Your sake, and let not anyone else have a share in them (i.e., in the intention). *(Al-Nasai)*

Return to this supplication often. Ask Allah to purify your intentions and guide your efforts so that every action brings you closer to Him.

PURE Practice

One Simple Micro-Practice

At the beginning of each day, pause for a moment and set a clear intention.

Quietly remind yourself:

Today I intend to carry out my responsibilities with sincerity, excellence and awareness of Allah.

This small practice takes only a few seconds, yet it can transform the way you approach your entire day. Because when intention becomes clear, direction follows.

CHAPTER TWO

Structure: Designing a Life That Supports Growth

Principle Introduction

Intention gives direction to a person's life.

Structure allows that direction to become reality.

Many people possess sincere intentions. They aim to grow spiritually, they want to contribute meaningfully to their communities, they want to create stability for their families and pursue excellence in their work. Yet without structure, even the strongest intentions struggle to sustain momentum.

Life naturally fills itself with responsibilities.

Meetings, commitments, family needs, unexpected demands and endless obligations can easily occupy every available moment. When structure is absent, these demands begin to dictate the rhythm of life rather than support it.

Structure is therefore not about rigidity.

It is about **design.**

A well-structured life creates space for what truly matters. It allows a woman to nurture her faith, invest in her growth, manage her duties and pursue her ambitions without feeling constantly overwhelmed by them.

For a Muslim woman striving for both dunya and akhirah, structure becomes an act of stewardship. It is the conscious decision to organise time, energy and priorities in a way that supports both spiritual strength and worldly responsibility.

Without structure, life becomes reactive.

With structure, life becomes intentional.

The PURE Connection

The Professional

Hakeema had always been someone who worked hard.

Over the years, she had built a respected reputation within her organisation. Her colleagues trusted her judgment. She managed complex projects well, which helped her gain positions of responsibility. At home, she carried just as much.

A wife.

A mother.

A daughter.

Someone her family relied on, in ways both seen and unseen.

Outwardly, she was progressing, fulfilling her responsibilities, showing up where she was needed. Yet beneath the surface, her days began to feel increasingly fragmented. Her mornings often started in a rush, preparing the children, responding to early messages, then quickly shifting from home tasks to work duties. Her days filled easily, meetings extended, tasks accumulated, and interruptions became constant.

By the time evening arrived, she felt mentally exhausted, yet her day was not finished. There were still responsibilities waiting at home, conversations to be had, and presence to be given. More than once, she found herself praying late at night, feeling as though the day had passed without pause, without stillness, without intention.

One evening, after a particularly demanding week, she stopped and reflected.

She had been busy, constantly moving, constantly responding. Yet she struggled to identify what had truly moved her forward.

The realisation was clear, she had discipline, she had capability.

What she lacked... was **structure.**

Her life had become reactive.

Shaped by what needed her most in the moment, rather than what mattered most overall.

That moment shifted something.

She began approaching her days with greater intention. She creating space for prayer, reflection and clarity before the day began.

She became more deliberate with her commitments at work and at home, recognising that not everything required her immediate response.

Gradually, the rhythm of her life began to change. The same responsibilities remained, but they no longer competed in the same way. Her work became focused, she was more intentional at home, her ibaadah (worship and good deeds) gained consistency again. She was no longer trying to manage everything. She was structuring her life to support what mattered. And through that structure, she found something she had been missing:

Clarity.

Space.

Direction.

Firdaws Reflection

Structure invites us to examine how our time and energy are currently organised. Consider the rhythm of your own life.

Reflect on the following:

- Which responsibilities currently consume the majority of your time?
- Do your daily routines support both your spiritual and personal growth?
- Where do you feel most overwhelmed or disorganised?
- Which areas of your life would benefit from clearer structure?

Sometimes, the problem isn't a lack of intention. It's that there aren't systems in place to support those intentions.

Awareness allows structure to begin.

Wisdom Unfolded

Islam consistently reminds believers that time is a trust.

Allah ﷻ swears by time in the Qur'an:

"By time, indeed, mankind is in loss, except for those who have believed and done righteous deeds and advised each other to the truth and advised each other to patience."
(Surah Al-Asr 103:1-3)

These verses remind us that time is not merely something we pass through. It is the very substance from which our lives are built.

Every day offers opportunities for growth, service, reflection and worship. Yet without conscious attention, these opportunities can easily pass unnoticed.

Structure allows a believer to honour time as the trust that it is.

By organising our lives intentionally, we ensure that our days reflect the values we hope to live by.

Principle in Action

Designing Your Personal Structure

A structured life does not appear overnight.

It is created through thoughtful design and small, consistent adjustments.

Use the following exercise to examine the structure of your current routines.

Step One — Observe Your Current Rhythm

Take a moment to consider how your time is currently spent across a typical week.

Reflect on the following:

- Which activities occupy the majority of your day?
- Which commitments bring genuine value or growth?
- Which responsibilities feel scattered, reactive or unnecessarily draining?

Observation helps reveal where structure may be missing.

Step Two — Identify Your Core Priorities

Now consider the areas of life that deserve consistent attention.

These may include:

- your relationship with Allah
- personal wellbeing
- professional responsibilities
- family and relationships
- personal development or learning

Ask yourself:

Does my current schedule reflect the priorities I claim to value?

If not, this is an opportunity to redesign your structure more intentionally.

Step Three — Design One Structural Shift

Rather than overhauling your entire routine, begin with one adjustment.

Examples may include:

- establishing a calm morning routine that begins with prayer and reflection
- creating focused work periods without distractions
- scheduling protected time for learning or personal growth
- ensuring regular moments for rest and renewal

Structure grows gradually.

Small intentional changes often produce the most sustainable transformation.

When structure supports your intentions, growth becomes easier to sustain.

Your efforts gain rhythm.

And your days begin to reflect the life you hope to build.

A Dua to Carry With You

Dua for barakah in time

اللَّهُمَّ بَارِكْ لِي فِي سَاعَتِي وَفِي يَوْمِي وَفِي عُمُرِي

Transliteration:

Allah ﷻ umma barik li fi sa'ati wa fi yawmi wa fi 'umri.

Translation:

O Allah ﷻ, bless my time, my day and my life. *(Al-Bukhari)*

Return to this supplication when your days begin to feel scattered or overwhelming.

Ask Allah to guide you. Seek a life rhythm that is productive, meaningful, and successful.

PURE Practice

One Simple Micro-Practice

Start each day with three quiet minutes to plan your intentions for the hours ahead.

Ask yourself:

- What are the three most important responsibilities I must honour today?

- When will I create space for prayer and reflection?
- What action today will move me closer to the life I hope to build?

This brief moment of planning can transform a reactive day into an intentional one.

Over time, these small moments of structure create a life that supports steady growth.

CHAPTER THREE

Wealth: Wealth as an Amanah

Principle Introduction

Wealth is one of the most misunderstood aspects of a Muslim woman's life. It can be viewed as a measure of status, comfort or success, while financial ambition can sometimes feel at odds with spiritual devotion. But in Islam, wealth is neither something to be glorified nor something to be feared.

It is a **trust.**

Every resource we have, financial, intellectual, relational, or otherwise is provision from Allah ﷻ. It carries responsibility. Wealth can support families, strengthen communities, create opportunities and enable a woman to contribute to something greater than herself.

How it is earned, managed and used therefore forms part of her accountability before Allah ﷻ. Seeing wealth as an amanah changes the way a woman approaches it. The question is no longer simply, How much can I earn?

It becomes: *"What am I building and how am I stewarding what Allah ﷻ has entrusted to me?"*

This is where wealth becomes more than accumulation. It becomes stewardship.

Stewardship means pursuing halal provision, managing resources wisely and directing financial growth towards purposes that benefit both dunya and akhirah.

But building wealth well requires more than pursuing growth. It requires first establishing a stable financial foundation.

Before investment strategies, additional income streams or long-term wealth creation become meaningful, there is a baseline every woman building wealth should establish.

The Financial Baseline is built on three foundations:

Stability — a stability fund set aside in a separate, easily accessible account, untouched except for genuine emergencies.

Freedom — reducing debt to zero, so that what you build is not continually being claimed by past obligations.

Income resilience — developing at least one source of income that is not dependent solely on a salary.

Until these foundations are established, growth strategies are being built on a less stable financial foundation.

The baseline is not the destination.

It is the foundation from which sustainable wealth can be built.

The PURE Connection

The Builder

As a pharmacist, Ayesha had developed a deep interest in Prophetic medicine and wanted to establish a small community project where she could help people reconnect with the Sunnah through the practical knowledge of using and making traditional remedies and growing herbs, spices and other natural resources.

Ayesha understood that what Allah ﷻ had entrusted to her with knowledge, resources and experience to create something that could continue benefiting others, so this became her legacy vision.

But when Ayesha looked at her finances, the dream felt out of reach. She had a steady job and a regular income, but she was not saving consistently. At the end of each month, she often wondered where her money had gone. Everyday spending had gradually accumulated, takeaway meals, subscriptions she barely used, convenience purchases and other small expenses that did not seem significant individually but added up over time.

She assumed that if she wanted to establish the project she had been dreaming about, she would need to earn significantly more.

Then someone challenged the way she was looking at everything. *What if the first step was not earning more, but understanding and structuring what she already had?* Ayesha decided to take an honest look at her finances.

For the first time, she could clearly see where her money was going. She identified the everyday spending she could reduce and the areas where she could save without significantly changing her lifestyle. More importantly, she made an intentional decision to start saving rather than simply saving whatever happened to be left at the end of the month.

She established separate savings for different purposes and began building her stability fund. She created a clear plan to pay off her outstanding debt and began thinking about how she could eventually develop an additional source of income that was not dependent solely on her salary.

Nothing about her income had changed except the way she managed it had.

As her system became more structured, she began saving consistently. Her emergency fund grew. Her debt balance began to fall. And because she had given her money purpose, she became much more aware of the decisions she was making with it.

When her debts were finally cleared, she redirected the money that had previously been going towards them into savings for her community project. Month after month, she continued saving with the same income she had always earned.

Years later, Ayesha looked back at what she had built. She realised that she had not needed a completely different financial life to begin with. She had needed to understand where her money was going, recognise where she could save, create a structure around it and give it a purpose and this was enough to begin.

The project that had once felt impossible was now something she was able to establish. Her income had not suddenly increased. Her circumstances had not dramatically changed. She had changed the way she stewarded what Allah ﷻ had already entrusted to her.

And that changed what became possible.

Firdaws Reflection

Wealth enters our lives in many ways , through professional growth, business opportunities, investments, savings and the resources we are entrusted with. But before thinking about how much more you can build, consider what you are building from.

A stronger financial foundation does not always begin with earning more. Sometimes, it begins by giving greater purpose and structure to what you already have.

Reflect:

- What does financial security mean to you and how secure d you currently feel?
- Which part of your financial baseline needs most attention?
- What legacy would you like to build?
- How could giving your money greater structure and purpose move you closer to that vision?

The goal is not simply to have more.

It is to build with intention, manage with responsibility and create a financial foundation strong enough to support what you are ultimately called to build.

Wisdom Unfolded

Allah ﷻ reminds believers that wealth is part of the trust placed in their care.

"Believe in Allah and His Messenger and spend out of that in which He has made you successors. For those who have believed among you and spent, there will be a great reward."
(Qur'an 57:7)

This verse reframes the way a believer views what they possess.

Rather than viewing wealth as something entirely their own, the believer recognises that they are entrusted with resources for a limited time. Their role is to manage those resources responsibly and to use them in ways that bring benefit.

This perspective encourages balance.

A Muslim is not discouraged from earning, building or investing. On the contrary, the pursuit of halal provision is honoured.

But wealth is never separated from accountability.

It remains connected to intention, integrity and generosity.

Principle in Action

Build Your Financial Foundation

Building wealth intentionally begins with understanding what you already have and creating a structure that supports where you want to go.

Use the following exercise to assess your position, establish your baseline and give your money purpose.

Step One — Understand Where You Are

Take an honest look at your current position and ask yourself:

- What comes into my household each month?
- Where does my money currently go?
- What am I spending unnecessarily?
- What savings do I currently have?
- What debts or financial obligations remain?
- Am I currently saving consistently?
- How dependent am I on one source of income?

Sometimes, the first financial shift does not come from earning more. It comes from finally seeing where your money is going.

Step Two — Establish Your Financial Baseline

Once you understand your current position, establish the foundations that make financial progress more sustainable.

Stability Fund: Build stability fund covering at least three months of essential living costs. Keep it separate and untouched except for genuine emergencies.

Debt: Identify your outstanding debts and create a clear plan to bring the balance to zero. As debts are cleared, the money that was previously being used to service them can be redirected towards saving, investing or the goals you are building towards.

Income Resilience: Begin developing at least one source of income that is not solely dependent on a salary. This may take time. The goal is to begin creating greater financial resilience rather than relying entirely on one source of income.

If one of these foundations is not yet established, that becomes your current financial priority.

The baseline is not the destination. It is the foundation from which sustainable wealth can be built.

Step Three — Give Your Money a Purpose

Once your foundation is becoming stronger, decide what you want your money to make possible. Think beyond simply having more in your bank account.

Ask yourself:

- What do I want my wealth to support?
- What would greater financial stability allow me to do?
- What do I want to provide for my family?
- How will I manage once I'm retired?
- What kind of legacy would I like my wealth to contribute towards?

Then give your savings a purpose. Rather than simply saving what is left, decide what you are saving for and create a structure that helps you move towards it.

Step Four — Redirect and Grow

Once your baseline is established, identify how you can continue building.

This could mean:

- Increasing your regular savings
- Improving your financial planning or budgeting
- Developing an additional income stream
- Exploring ethical investment opportunities
- Building assets for long-term stability
- Increasing your charitable giving

Choose one action that moves you closer to the financial future you have identified. Start by giving what you already have greater structure, intention and purpose.

Wealth grows best when pursued intentionally and managed responsibly. When we see wealth as an amanah, financial growth becomes about more than personal gain. It becomes a means of serving others, strengthening communities, and building lasting benefits.

A Dua to Carry With You

Dua for Support

اللَّهُمَّ أَكْثِرْ مَالِي، وَوَلَدِي، وَبَارِكْ لِي فِيمَا أَعْطَيْتَنِي وَأَطِلْ حَيَاتِي عَلَى طَاعَتِكَ، وَأَحْسِنْ عَمَلِي وَاغْفِرْ لِي

Transliteration:
Allahumma akthir mali wa waladi, wa barik-li fima a'taitani [wa atil hayati 'ala ta'atik, wa ahsin 'amali wagfirli]

Translation:
O Allah, increase my wealth and offspring and bless me in what You have provided for me and give me a long life in obedience to You and help me to do all that is good and forgive me (*Al-Bukhari)*

This supplication reminds the believer that all provision comes from Allah ﷻ alone, so we seek His blessing and guidance in it to live a life of worldly stability and spiritual success.

PURE Practice

One Simple Micro-Practice

Once a week, review your finances with intentional awareness.

Ask yourself:

- Is my income being earned in ways that align with my values?
- Am I managing what I have responsibly?
- What small step can I take this week to strengthen my financial stewardship?

Even brief moments of financial reflection can cultivate greater clarity, responsibility and purpose in how wealth is built and used.

CHAPTER FOUR

Legacy: Building What Outlives You

Principle Introduction

Many people spend their lives focusing on what must be achieved in the present.

Responsibilities demand attention. Opportunities appear and require effort. Goals form around the needs of the moment, building careers, supporting families and creating stability.

These pursuits are important.

Yet a life shaped only by immediate priorities can sometimes overlook a deeper question:

What will remain after I am gone?

Legacy invites a person to step beyond the urgency of the present and consider the long-term impact of their actions.

Within the Islamic tradition, legacy is not measured by recognition or status. It is measured by benefit, the ways in which a person's actions continue to bring goodness long after their lifetime has ended.

Knowledge shared with sincerity.

A charity that continues to serve others.

Children raised with strong values.

Projects and initiatives that uplift communities.

Each of these represents a form of legacy.

For a Muslim woman striving to live intentionally, legacy becomes an extension of purpose. It shapes how she invests her time, how she directs her resources and how she contributes to the world around her.

When viewed through this lens, the question is no longer simply:

What am I building today?

It becomes:

What am I building that will continue to benefit others tomorrow?

The PURE Connection

The Visionary

Aseela had always been someone who thought about the future.

She worked hard throughout her career. She advanced in her field while also supporting her family. At the same time, she kept strong ties in her community. She had built stability through years of consistent effort.

Yet one evening during a community gathering, a conversation sparked a deeper reflection.

An older woman spoke about a school that had been founded decades earlier by a small group of families want to make sure the next generation would have access to both education and faith-centred guidance.

Many of those original founders had long since passed away.

But the school continued to grow.

Hundreds of children had passed through its classrooms, benefiting from something that had been built many years before.

As Aseela listened, a quiet thought settled in her mind.

The people who had started that school had likely lived ordinary lives filled with responsibilities and challenges, much like her own. Yet the choices they made had created something that continued to benefit others long after their time in this world had ended.

That evening, Aseela found herself reflecting on a question she had rarely asked before:

What will remain from the life I am building?

Her work mattered. Her responsibilities were meaningful.

But legacy invited her to think beyond the present moment.

She began considering how her resources, knowledge and opportunities might contribute to something that could continue benefiting others in the years to come. Not necessarily through grand gestures, but through intentional choices made over time.

In that moment, her perspective shifted. Success was no longer measured only by what she accomplished during her lifetime.

It was also shaped by what she helped create for the future.

Firdaws Reflection

Legacy begins with reflection on the long-term impact of our actions.

Consider the following questions:

- When you think about the future, what kind of impact would you hope your life leaves behind?

- Which values or contributions would you want others to remember you for?
- Are there causes, projects or forms of service that resonate deeply with you?
- How might your current resources, skills or opportunities contribute to something that benefits others over time?

Legacy does not require extraordinary circumstances. It begins with intentional choices repeated consistently.

Wisdom Unfolded

The Prophet ﷺ reminded believers that the impact of a person's actions can extend beyond their lifetime.

"When a person dies, their deeds come to an end except for three: ongoing charity, beneficial knowledge or a righteous child who prays for them."
(Muslim)

This narration beautifully captures the essence of legacy. It reminds us that the most meaningful contributions are those that continue to bring benefit even after a person's life has concluded.

These contributions may appear simple in the moment, teaching someone knowledge, supporting a charitable cause or raising children with sincerity and faith.

Yet over time, their impact multiplies.

A believer who understands this begins to view their actions differently.

They recognise that even small contributions can become part of something far greater than themselves.

Principle in Action

Designing Your Legacy Vision

Legacy is rarely built through a single moment. It develops gradually through intentional choices and long-term thinking.

Use the following exercise to explore what legacy could mean within your own life.

Step One — Define What Matters Most

Reflect on the values and contributions that feel most meaningful to you.

Ask yourself:

- What causes or areas of service resonate deeply with my heart?
- Which forms of contribution would I feel proud to support over the long term?
- What kind of positive change would I hope to see within my family, community or the wider Ummah?

This step clarifies where your efforts may be most impactful.

Step Two — Identify Your Existing Resources

Legacy is not limited to financial wealth.

Consider the resources already available to you:

- knowledge and experience
- professional skills
- relationships and networks
- financial resources
- time and mentorship

Each of these can contribute to long-term benefit.

Step Three — Begin With One Intentional Contribution

Choose one area where you can begin contributing with consistency.

Examples may include:

- mentoring someone in your field
- supporting educational or charitable initiatives
- sharing beneficial knowledge
- establishing a regular charity
- contributing to community projects

Legacy begins with small, intentional acts that are sustained over time.

When repeated consistently, these acts become part of a story that continues long after we are gone.

A Dua to Carry With You

Dua for knowledge, provision and accepted deeds

اللَّهُمَّ إِنِّي أَسْأَلُكَ عِلْمًا نَافِعًا، وَرِزْقًا طَيِّبًا، وَعَمَلًا مُتَقَبَّلًا

Transliteration:

Allāhumma innī as'aluka ʿilman nāfiʿan, wa rizqan ṭayyiban, wa ʿamalan mutaqabbalan

Translation:

O Allah, I ask You for beneficial knowledge, good provision and accepted deeds. (Ibn Majah)

Through this supplication, we ask Allah ﷻ to grant what we need to build a lasting legacy of good in this life and in the next.

PURE Practice

One Simple Micro-Practice

Choose one small act of ongoing charity that you can begin this week.

This may include:

- supporting an educational initiative
- contributing to a charitable cause regularly

- sharing knowledge that benefits others
- mentoring someone who seeks guidance

The size of the action matters far less than the consistency behind it.

Over time, even small acts can become part of a legacy that continues to bring reward long after a person's lifetime has ended.

PART TWO

UNITY

Strength Through Belonging

وَٱعْتَصِمُوا۟ بِحَبْلِ ٱللَّهِ جَمِيعًا وَلَا تَفَرَّقُوا۟ ۚ ... ١٠٣

'And hold firmly to the rope of Allah all together and do not become divided.'

Surah Ali-'Imran 3:103

True strength is found when hearts are united in faith, purpose and sincere care for one another.

PURE INTRODUCTION

UNITY

Strength Through Belonging

A life built with purpose does not exist in isolation.

Our intentions, discipline, wealth and a aspirations for legacy all shape the way we live. Yet even the most intentional life cannot be built alone.

Human beings are created for connection. We are shaped by the people around us, strengthened by those who support us, and influenced by those who walk alongside us.

Our growth is therefore not only personal. It is deeply connected to the relationships we nurture, the communities belong to, and the environments we create around ourselves.

Unity extends beyond the people in our lives.

It also asks us to consider the environments we move through daily - the spaces, relationships and communities that either support the life we are building or quietly pulls us away from it.

Unity carries even greater meaning for a Muslim woman committed to both dunya and akhirah. She is not only an individual striving for her own development. She is part of a wider Ummah, a collective bound by faith, responsibility and shared purpose.

Unity, therefore, becomes a discipline.

It is the conscious effort to build relationships that strengthen faith, to create environments that support growth and to contribute to something greater than oneself.

Without unity, even the most capable individual can feel isolated.

Without support, growth can become difficult to sustain.

Without meaningful connection, opportunities for impact remain limited.

But when unity is present, strength multiplies.

A supportive environment can elevate a person beyond what they might achieve alone. A strong network can open doors that effort alone cannot access. A sense of belonging can provide stability through seasons of both growth and challenge.

Unity is not simply about being surrounded by others.

It is about intentional connection.

It is about knowing who you are, choosing the environments that shape you and contributing in ways that uplift those around you.

Within the PURE Framework, Unity is expressed through four principles:

Grounding — Understanding who you are through the lens of faith

Support — Building relationships that sustain you through every season

Network — Creating intentional connections that expand opportunity

Contribution — Using your capacity to uplift others and strengthen the Ummah

Together, these principles ensure that growth is not experienced alone, but shared, strengthened and multiplied.

Because a life of faith, wealth and legacy is built through connection.

CHAPTER FIVE

Grounding: Tawheed-Centred Self-Understanding

Principle Introduction

Before a person can build strong relationships with others, they must first understand who they are.

Not through the expectations placed upon them, nor through the roles they occupy, but through a deeper, more stable lens.

In Islam, that lens is Tawheed.

Tawheed is the foundation for identity. It shapes how a person understands their worth, their purpose and their place in the world. It reminds the believer that their value is not defined by achievement, recognition or comparison, but by their relationship with Allah ﷻ.

Without this grounding, identity can become unstable.

A person may begin to define themselves through external validation, success, approval, social expectations or the opinions of others. Over time, this creates a subtle form of dependence, where self-worth rises and falls based on factors that are constantly changing.

Grounding restores stability. It allows a woman to anchor her identity in something unchanging, her faith, her purpose and her relationship with the One who created her.

From that place, decisions become clearer.

Boundaries become easier to uphold.

Relationships become healthier because they are no longer driven by the need for validation but by intention and sincerity.

Grounding is therefore about standing within the world with clarity of identity.

The PURE Connection

The Seeker

Sakina had always adapted easily to the environments she found herself in. At work, she was known for her professionalism and ability to meet expectations. Within her family, she carried responsibility with care, often placing the needs of others before her own. Among friends, she adjusted her tone, her interests and sometimes even her opinions to maintain harmony. She was thoughtful. She was considerate. She was well-liked.

Yet over time, she began to notice something she could not ignore.

In different spaces, she felt like a slightly different version of herself.

The changes were subtle, almost unnoticeable to others. But internally, they created a quiet sense of disconnection.

One evening, after a conversation in which she had agreed with something that did not sit comfortably with her, she found herself reflecting more deeply than usual.

It was not the conversation itself that stayed with her.

It was the realisation that she had responded automatically, without pausing to consider whether her response reflected what she truly believed.

Later that night, as she prepared for prayer, a question surfaced in her mind:

Who am I when no one is expecting anything from me?

The question lingered.

She realised that much of her identity had been shaped by adapting to expectations, meeting standards, maintaining harmony and fulfilling roles.

None of these was inherently wrong, but they had slowly distanced her from a clearer understanding of herself.

In the days that followed, she began to reflect more intentionally.

She revisited what she believed, what she valued and what she wanted her life to reflect, not through the lens of others, but through her relationship with Allah ﷻ.

Gradually, something began to settle within her, her sense of self became quieter, but more certain. From that clarity, her interactions with others began to change.

Firdaws Reflection

Grounding invites you to return to your centre.

Take a moment to reflect:

- In which areas of your life do you feel most like yourself?
- Where do you find yourself adjusting to meet expectations?
- How much of your identity is shaped by external validation?
- What does your faith teach you about your worth and purpose?

True grounding begins when identity is no longer shaped by shifting expectations, but by a stable foundation.

Wisdom Unfolded

Allah ﷻ reminds us of the purpose for which we were created:

"And I did not create jinn and mankind except to worship Me."
(Qur'an 51:56)

This verse provides a profound anchor for identity.

It reminds the believer that their primary purpose is not defined by roles, achievements or external recognition, but by their relationship with Allah ﷻ.

When this understanding is internalised, it reshapes how a person views themselves.

Their worth is no longer dependent on outcomes.

Their identity is no longer fragmented across different environments.

Instead, it becomes unified, rooted in a single, unchanging truth.

Principle in Action

Anchoring Your Identity

Grounding your identity requires intentional reflection and conscious realignment.

Use the following exercise to strengthen your sense of self through the lens of faith.

Step One — Recognise External Influences

Take time to identify the influences that shape how you see yourself.

Reflect on:

- expectations from family, work or social environments
- cultural or societal standards
- comparisons with others

Ask yourself:

Which of these influences align with my values, and which may be shaping me without awareness?

Step Two — Reconnect With Core Beliefs

Now return to what anchors you.

Reflect on:

- your relationship with Allah ﷻ
- the values your faith encourages you to uphold
- the kind of person you strive to be before Allah

Ask yourself:

If I were to define myself through my faith, what would that look like?

Step Three — Align One Area of Your Life

Choose one area where your actions or responses may not fully reflect your values.

This could be:

- how you communicate in certain environments
- how you set boundaries
- how you make decisions under pressure

Ask yourself:

What would it look like to respond from a place of grounded identity rather than expectation?

Begin with one small shift.

Over time, these shifts create a stronger and more consistent sense of self.

When identity is grounded, relationships become healthier, decisions become clearer, and the need for external validation begins to fade.

A Dua to Carry With You

Dua for a firm heart

يَا مُقَلِّبَ الْقُلُوبِ ثَبِّتْ قَلْبِي عَلَى دِينِكَ

Transliteration:

Yaa Muqallibal Quloob Thabbit Qalbee 'alaa Deenik.

Translation:

"Oh, turner of the hearts (Allah ﷻ, the Most High), keep our hearts firm on your religion " *(At-Tirmidhi)*

The Prophet ﷺ often prayed for this, reminding us that we should always ask Allah for a stable heart.

PURE Practice

One Simple Micro-Practice

Pause once during your day and ask yourself:

Am I acting from clarity or from expectation?

This brief moment of awareness can help you reconnect with your goals. Over time, it will boost your ability to navigate life with a steady sense of self.

CHAPTER SIX

Support: Strength Through Support Systems

Principle Introduction

Strength is often misunderstood.

It is often linked to independence, the ability to carry responsibility alone, to face challenges without visible stress and to continue giving without expecting anything in return.

Many women become known for this kind of strength.

They are dependable. Capable. Resilient.

They support others with consistency, often without hesitation.

Yet over time, this form of strength can become isolating.

When a woman is always the one others turn to, she might feel like she has to manage everything alone. Asking for support may feel unfamiliar, or even uncomfortable.

But within the Islamic tradition, strength is not defined by isolation.

It is strengthened through connection.

The Prophet ﷺ himself was supported by his family, his companions and his community. His life reflects the importance of companionship, mutual care and shared responsibility.

Support is therefore not a weakness.

It is a structure that sustains growth.

For a Muslim woman focused on a life of faith, wealth and legacy, support systems are vital. They offer emotional support, practical help, and spiritual encouragement in every season of life.

Without support, even the most capable individual can experience strain.

With support, growth becomes more sustainable.

The PURE Connection

The Caregiver

Nasira had always been the one people turned to.

Within her family, she was the one who organised, supported and ensured that everything ran smoothly. Among her friends, she was the one who listened, advised and showed up without hesitation. At work, she was known for her reliability and willingness to take on responsibility. In every space she entered, she became someone others could rely on. She carried it all with quiet strength and for a long time, she rarely questioned it.

Gradually, she began to feel the weight of it. Her days were filled with giving, her time, her energy, her attention. Yet, in quieter moments, something felt unspoken, a sense of depletion. Not because she resented what she gave, but because she rarely experienced that same depth of support in return.

One afternoon, after a particularly demanding week, a colleague asked her a simple question:

"Who do you go to when you need support?"

The question caught her off guard.

She paused, searching for an answer that did not immediately come.

She had family, friends, and connections around her, but when she looked closer, she noticed something deeper.

She was surrounded...

But not necessarily supported.

Her relationships were built around her being the one who gave.

The one who held space.

The one who remained strong.

She had become so accustomed to this role that she had never fully allowed herself to be seen in need.

In many ways, supporting others had become a form of protection, a way to stay occupied, a way to avoid acknowledging what was missing. That realisation was uncomfortable, but it was honest.

Moving forward, she began to approach her relationships differently. She allowed herself to be more open. More honest. Less composed.

She began to notice which relationships created space for her and which did not.

Slowly, she started building something she had not intentionally built before: Mutual support. The shift was not immediate, but it was meaningful. For the first time, she no longer felt as though she had to carry everything alone. In that space, something changed. Her strength did not weaken, it deepened.

Firdaws Reflection

Support begins with awareness.

Reflect on the role you currently play within your relationships:

- Are you often the one others rely on?
- Do you feel comfortable asking for support when you need it?
- Which relationships in your life feel mutually supportive?
- Where might you be giving more than you are able to sustain?

Support is not only about who you give to.

It is also about who you allow to support you.

Wisdom Unfolded

Allah ﷻ reminds believers of the strength found in unity:

"The believers are but brothers, so make a settlement between your brothers. And fear Allah that you may receive mercy."
(Qur'an 49:10)

This verse reflects the spirit of mutual care within the Ummah.

Believers are not meant to exist in isolation. They are meant to support, uplift and strengthen one another.

The Prophet ﷺ also demonstrated the importance of companionship, surrounding himself with those who provided support, counsel and encouragement.

These examples remind us that seeking and offering support is part of a balanced and healthy life.

Principle in Action

Strengthening Your Support System

Support systems are built intentionally.

Use the following exercise to evaluate and strengthen the relationships that surround you.

Step One — Identify Your Current Circles

Consider the different relationships in your life.

You may find it helpful to think in layers:

- Inner circle: Husband, best friends and close family members you trust completely, providing deep emotional support, intimacy and a strong sense of security.

- Stability circle: Close friends and extended family who offer consistent support, shared experiences and reliable connections in everyday life.
- Growth circle: Mentors, role models or peers who challenge your thinking and inspire personal development and progress.
- Wider network: Acquaintances, colleagues and community members who broaden your perspective, create opportunities and support light social connections.

Reflect on where your current relationships sit.

Step Two — Assess Balance Within Your Relationships

Ask yourself:

- Which relationships feel mutually supportive?
- Where do I consistently give without receiving support?
- Are there relationships that drain my energy without contributing to my growth?

This step is not about judgement. It is about awareness.

Step Three — Strengthen One Supportive Connection

Choose one relationship that you would like to nurture more intentionally.

This could involve:

- initiating a more meaningful conversation
- sharing honestly about your current experiences
- spending intentional time together
- asking for support when needed

Support grows through consistency and openness.

When support systems are strong, they create a foundation that allows you to give, grow and navigate challenges with greater ease.

A Dua to Carry With You

Dua for good companionship

اللَّهُمَّ إِنِّي أَسْأَلُكَ حُبَّكَ، وَحُبَّ مَنْ يُحِبُّكَ، وَالْعَمَلَ الَّذِي يُبَلِّغُنِي حُبَّكَ، اللَّهُمَّ اجْعَلْ حُبَّكَ أَحَبَّ إِلَيَّ مِنْ نَفْسِي وَأَهْلِي وَمِنَ الْمَاءِ الْبَارِدِ

Transliteration:

Allāhumma innī as'aluka ḥubbaka, wa ḥubba man yuḥibbuka, wa al-ʿamala alladhī yuballighunī ḥubbaka, Allāhumma aj'al ḥubbaka aḥabba ilayya min nafsī wa ahli wa minal-mā'il bārid.

Translation:

O Allah, I ask You for Your love and the love of whoever loves You, and the deeds that will bring me closer to Your love. O Allah, make Your love more beloved to me than myself, my family and cold water. *(Al-Tirmidhi)*

This supplication not only asks Allah ﷻ to fill our hearts with His love but to connect us with people and actions that nurture us and help us to grow in goodness.

PURE Practice

One Simple Micro-Practice

Reach out to one trusted person this week and share something honestly.

It could be:

- something you are navigating
- a challenge you are facing
- a need for support
- or simply a moment of connection

Allowing yourself to be supported is a step toward building stronger, more balanced relationships.

CHAPTER SEVEN

Network: Building Relationships That Expand Opportunity

Principle Introduction

Relationships shape the direction of a person's life in ways that are often underestimated.

While support systems offer emotional and personal stability, networks influence exposure, access and opportunity. They determine the environments a person is part of, the conversations they are included in and the doors that may open over time.

Yet many people approach networking with hesitation. It can feel transactional, insincere or uncomfortable, particularly when it is framed purely as a means of personal gain.

Within the PURE Framework, networking is not approached in this way.

It is approached with intention and integrity.

A meaningful network is not built through opportunistic interactions. It is cultivated through genuine relationships, shared values and mutual respect. It is formed by connecting with people who inspire growth, expand perspective and create opportunities for collective advancement.

For a sister building a life of faith, wealth and legacy, networks play a significant role.

They drive professional growth, create pathways for collaboration and foster spaces where ideas can turn into impactful initiatives.

Without intentional networks, opportunities can remain limited.

With them, growth can expand beyond what effort alone can achieve.

The PURE Connection

The Connector

Anisah had built her business with intention.

She was consistent, disciplined and deeply committed to the quality of what she offered. Her work reflected care, thought and integrity.

Over time, she created something solid, but it wasn't growing. Not in the way she expected. There were moments where she paused and questioned it. She was doing everything she had been taught to do:

Refining her offer.

Improving her systems.

Staying committed to her work.

Yet opportunities felt limited. Growth felt contained. And despite her effort, her business seemed to remain within the same boundaries.

She began to notice something.

It wasn't her lack of capability, it her lack of connection. The women whose businesses were expanding were not only skilled. They were visible. They were connected. They were part of conversations, collaborations and spaces where opportunities were shared, created and extended.

Anisah realised she had built her business in isolation. She had focused on the work. But she had not invested in the environment around it.

That shift changed how she approached her growth. She began to show up more intentionally. Not to promote, but to connect. She engaged in spaces aligned with her values. She built relationships with women who were also building. She shared her work more openly, without hesitation. As her environment changed, new pathways began to open. Conversations led to opportunities, relationships led to collaboration and visibility led to expansion.

Her work had always been strong, now, it was supported.

Seen.

Connected.

Positioned to grow.

And for the first time, her business began to move beyond what she could build alone.

Firdaws Reflection

Networking begins with awareness of how relationships influence opportunity.

Reflect on the following:

- Are you intentionally building relationships beyond your immediate responsibilities?
- Which environments or spaces are you currently part of?

- Where might opportunities exist that you are not yet exposed to?
- How comfortable are you with engaging in new conversations or expanding your network?

A strong network is not built by chance.

It is built through intentional presence and meaningful connection.

Wisdom Unfolded

The Prophet ﷺ emphasised the importance of maintaining and nurturing relationships.

"Anyone who wants to have his provision expanded and his term of life prolonged should maintain ties of kinship."
(Bukhari & Muslim)

This hadith highlights a powerful connection between relationships and provision. While it directly refers to family ties, its broader message reflects the value placed on maintaining strong, sincere connections. Relationships are not separate from provision; they are often part of the means through which Allah ﷻ expands it.

When approached with sincerity and good character, connections can become a source of both worldly opportunity and spiritual reward.

Principle in Action

Building Your Network With Intention

A meaningful network is built gradually through consistent and intentional effort.

Use the following exercise to begin strengthening your connections.

Step One — Map Your Current Network

Consider the people you are currently connected to across different areas of your life:

- professional connections
- community connections
- mentors or advisors
- peers who share similar goals

Ask yourself:

Which of these relationships actively support my growth?

Step Two — Identify Areas for Expansion

Now consider where growth opportunities may exist.

Reflect on:

- industries or fields you would like to grow within
- communities aligned with your values
- individuals whose work or mindset inspires you

Ask yourself:

Where would it be beneficial for me to build new connections?

Step Three — Take One Intentional Step

Choose one simple action to expand your network.

This could include:

- initiating a meaningful conversation
- attending a gathering or event
- reaching out to someone whose work you respect
- contributing to a shared space or community

Networking does not require large gestures.

It grows through consistent, thoughtful interaction.

When relationships are built with sincerity and intention, they become a source of opportunity, collaboration and long-term growth.

A Dua to Carry With You

Dua for beneficial actions

اللَّهُمَّ اهْدِنِي لِأَحْسَنِ الْأَخْلَاقِ، وَاجعلني سببًا في نفعِ الآخرين

Transliteration:

Allāhumma ihdinī li-aḥsani al-akhlāq, waj'alnī sababān fī naf'i al-ākhirīn

Translation:

O Allah, guide me to the best of character, and make me a means of benefit to others. *(Muslim)*

Return to this supplication as a reminder to build strong character and become a source of benefit within your relationships and circles.

PURE Practice

One Simple Micro-Practice

Initiate one intentional connection this week.

This could be:

- reaching out to someone you admire
- reconnecting with someone you have not spoken to in some time
- engaging more actively in a professional or community space

Focus on sincerity rather than outcome.

Over time, these small steps build a network that supports both your growth and your contribution.

CHAPTER EIGHT

Contribution: Using Your Capacity to Uplift Others

Principle Introduction

Growth reaches its fullest meaning when it extends beyond the individual.

A person may develop clarity, build structure, accumulate resources and surround themselves with strong relationships. Yet without contribution, that growth remains contained.

Contribution transforms personal development into a collective benefit.

Within the Islamic tradition, a believer is not only concerned with their own progress but with the well-being of others. Their knowledge, time, skills and resources are all seen as opportunities to bring benefit where it is needed.

Contribution does not require perfection, nor does it require abundance.

It begins with recognising that every individual has been given something of value, whether knowledge, experience, access, time or resources and that these can be used to uplift others.

For a Muslim woman building a life of faith, wealth and legacy, contribution becomes a natural extension of growth.

It is the point where intention becomes impact.

Where what she has built begins to serve something greater than herself.

The PURE Connection

The Visionary

Kareema had always been aware of the needs within her community.

Through her work and personal experiences, she often encountered situations where people lacked access to opportunities she once had, including guidance, education and mentorship.

For a long time, she noticed these gaps quietly.

She assumed that meaningful change required significant resources, large platforms or perfect timing, things she felt she did not yet have.

So she continued focusing on her own responsibilities, telling herself that perhaps one day she would be in a position to contribute more meaningfully.

But one conversation shifted her perspective.

A younger woman approached her after a small gathering and asked a simple question about navigating early career decisions.

The conversation was brief.

But it was sincere.

And as Kareema offered her thoughts, she realised something she had previously overlooked.

What felt ordinary to her, her experiences, her lessons, her perspective, held value for someone else.

She began to reconsider what contribution was required.

It did not begin with scale, it began with willingness.

In the weeks that followed, she started small.

She made herself more available for conversations. She shared insights more openly. She offered guidance where she could, without waiting for the “perfect” moment.

Gradually, these small actions began to grow.

What started as occasional conversations developed into something more structured, opportunities to support, guide and uplift others in ways she had once thought were beyond her reach.

Her life became more purposeful because what she had built was no longer only serving her, it had began to serve others.

Firdaws Reflection

Contribution begins with recognising what you already have.

Reflect on the following:

- What knowledge, skills or experiences have you gained through your journey?
- In what ways could these benefit others?
- Are there needs within your community that you feel drawn toward?
- What has held you back from contributing more intentionally?

Often, the barrier is not a lack of ability.

It is the assumption that we must wait until we have more.

Wisdom Unfolded

The Prophet ﷺ said:

"The most beloved people to Allah are those who are most beneficial to others."
(Tabarani)

This hadith reframes the concept of success. It reminds us that true value is not only found in personal achievement, but in the benefit we bring to others.

Contribution, therefore, is not an optional addition to a meaningful life, it is a central part of it. Even small acts, offering guidance, sharing knowledge, supporting someone in need, carry weight when done with sincerity.

Principle in Action

Activating Your Contribution

Contribution becomes sustainable when it is approached with clarity and intention.

Use the following exercise to begin translating your capacity into meaningful impact.

Step One — Identify Your Zone of Contribution

Reflect on where your strengths and experiences intersect with the needs around you.

Ask yourself:

- What do people often come to me for?
- What challenges have I navigated that others may benefit from learning about?
- Which areas of service feel most meaningful to me?

Your zone of contribution often lies where your experience meets someone else's need.

Step Two — Remove the Barrier of Scale

Many people delay contribution because they believe it must be large to be meaningful.

Challenge this assumption.

Ask yourself:

What is one small way I could begin contributing right now?

This could include:

- offering guidance to someone earlier in their journey
- sharing knowledge or resources
- supporting a community initiative
- volunteering time or skills

Impact grows through consistency, not scale.

Step Three — Commit to One Consistent Action

Choose one form of contribution that you can sustain.

Consistency transforms small actions into meaningful impact.

When repeated over time, even simple contributions can reach far beyond what we initially expect.

Contribution shifts the focus from what am I building? to who is benefiting from what I build?

And in that shift, growth takes on deeper meaning.

A Dua to Carry With You

Dua for amanah and rightful responsibility

اللَّهُمَّ اجعلني أمينًا على ما ائتمنتني، ووفّقني لما تحب وترضى، وارزقني أن أُؤدّي مسؤوليّتي بحقّ

Transliteration:

Allāhumma aj'alnī amīnan 'alā mā u'tumintanī, wa waffiqnī limā tuḥibbu wa tarda, wa arzuqnī an ū'addī mas'ūliyyatī bi-ḥaqq

Translation:

O Allah, make me trustworthy over that which You have entrusted to me, grant me success in that which You love and are pleased with and provide me the ability to fulfil my responsibilities properly. *(Muslim & Ahmad)*

This supplication reflects the desire to be a trustworthy source through which goodness benefits others and the wider community.

PURE Practice

One Simple Micro-Practice

Offer one intentional act of benefit this week.

It could be:

- guiding someone who seeks advice

- sharing something beneficial you have learned
- supporting someone quietly
- contributing to a cause

Do it sincerely, without expectation.

Small acts, when done consistently, become part of a legacy of impact.

PART THREE

Reputation

Influence Built With Integrity

يَـٰٓأَيُّهَا ٱلَّذِينَ ءَامَنُوا۟ ٱتَّقُوا۟ ٱللَّهَ وَقُولُوا۟ قَوْلًا سَدِيدًا ٧٠

'O you who have believed, fear Allah and speak words of appropriate justice.'

Surah Al-Ahzab 33:70

A life of integrity begins with truthfulness in word, sincerity in intention and responsibility in action.

PURE INTRODUCTION

REPUTATION

The Influence of a Life Lived With Integrity

As a woman grows in clarity, structure and connection, something starts to change. Her presence becomes felt, her words carry weight, her actions influence others and her decisions begin to extend beyond her immediate environment.

Whether she intends it or not, she becomes visible and with visibility comes responsibility.

Reputation is not built through what a person claims, it is formed through what they consistently embody. It is shaped in quiet moments, in the decisions made when no one is watching, in the standards upheld when compromise would be easier and in the way a person carries themselves across different spaces.

For a Muslim woman, reputation is not about performance, it is about alignment - the natural outcome of character, conduct and capability reflecting the values of her faith. It extends beyond professional presence: it includes how she carries herself, sustains her health, and allows her daily rhythms to reflect care for the body entrusted to her.

As her professional and personal presence expands, so does her influence. People begin to observe more closely. They listen more carefully. They take cues, not only from what she says, but from how she lives.

This is where intention must deepen because influence, when not anchored, can easily become driven by validation or external approval. When grounded in faith, it becomes a responsibility, a means of representing values, a way of guiding others through example and creating impact beyond words.

Within the PURE Framework, Reputation is expressed through four principles:

Brand — Presenting an identity that reflects your values

Influence — Using your voice with clarity and responsibility

Integrity — Aligning your actions with your beliefs

Authority — Building trust through consistency and credibility

Together, these principles shape how a woman is seen, trusted and remembered. Reputation is ultimately about what you represent.

CHAPTER NINE

Brand: An Identity That Reflects Your Deen

Principle Introduction

Every person communicates something before they even speak.

Their presence, conduct and demeanour create an impression. Over time, that impression becomes associated with who they are.

This is their **brand.**

In many spaces, branding is often reduced to appearance, how a person looks, presents themselves or curates their image. While these elements may play a role, they do not define the essence of a person's identity.

A brand, in its truest sense, is not constructed, it is revealed.

It is the outward expression of what a person consistently believes, values and embodies.

For a woman of faith, this expression is anchored in her deen.

Her identity is not shaped solely by trends, expectations or external validation. It is shaped by her understanding of who she is before Allah ﷻ, and the values she chooses to uphold in every space she enters.

This does not mean she withdraws from professional or social environments, rather, it means she shows up within them with clarity.

Her presence reflects intention.

Her communication reflects thoughtfulness.

Her conduct reflects integrity.

Over time, this consistency forms a reputation that is both authentic and trustworthy.

Brand, therefore, is not about creating a version of yourself that is appealing to others.

It is about ensuring that what people see aligns with what you stand for.

The PURE Connection

The Professional

Sharifah had recently stepped into a new role within her organisation.

It was an opportunity she had worked towards for years, one that brought greater responsibility, visibility and influence. She was now interacting with senior colleagues, representing her team in important discussions and contributing to decisions that carried weight.

With this shift came a heightened awareness of how she was perceived. In meetings, she noticed how others presented themselves, the confidence in their communication, the clarity in their ideas and the way they positioned their expertise.

At times, she found herself questioning how she should present herself in these spaces.

Should she adjust her tone to match the environment?

Should she present herself in a way that aligned more closely with what others expected?

Should she prioritise fitting in or standing firm in what she valued?

These questions were subtle, but persistent. She wanted to be taken seriously. She wanted to be respected but she also wanted to remain aligned with who she was.

One afternoon, after a meeting where she felt she had held back more than she intended, she paused to reflect.

She realised that her uncertainty was not about capability, it was about clarity. She had spent years developing her skills, but she had not fully defined how she wanted to show up.

What did she want her presence to represent?

What values did she want to be known for?

What would it look like to be both professional and fully aligned with her identity?

That reflection marked a shift.

Instead of trying to adapt to every environment, she began to define her own standard.

She became more intentional in how she communicated, ensuring her words reflected both confidence and sincerity. She carried herself with quiet assurance, grounded in her values rather than shaped by comparison.

Over time, something became evident, she did not need to fit into every space. Her clarity allowed her to stand within those spaces with consistency and that consistency began to shape how she was recognised and respected.

Firdaws Reflection

Your brand is formed through consistency.

Reflect on the following:

- What do you want to be known for?
- Which values guide how you present yourself in different spaces?
- Do you feel consistent in how you show up across environments?
- Where might you be adjusting yourself to meet expectations?

Your brand is not defined by a single moment.

It is shaped by repeated patterns of behaviour.

Wisdom Unfolded

The Prophet ﷺ said:

"I was sent to perfect good character."
(Ahmad)

This hadith reminds us that character is central to how a believer is recognised.

The way a person conducts themselves, their honesty, their humility, their consistency, becomes part of how they are known.

In this sense, a believer's "brand" is not separate from their character.

It is an extension of it.

When a character is strong, the impression a person leaves naturally reflects it.

Principle in Action

Designing Your Personal Brand

A strong and authentic brand begins with clarity.

Use the following exercise to define how you want to be perceived and what your presence represents.

Step One — Identify Your Core Values

Reflect on the values that guide your decisions and behaviour.

These may include:

- integrity
- sincerity
- professionalism
- excellence
- humility

Ask yourself:

Which of these values do I consistently embody, and which require strengthening?

Step Two — Define How You Want to Be Known

Consider how others currently perceive you, and how you would like to be perceived.

Reflect on:

- what people associate with your name
- how you communicate and present yourself

- the impression you leave after interactions

Ask yourself:

Does this align with the values I want to represent?

Step Three — Align Your Presence With Your Values

Choose one area where you can strengthen alignment.

This could include:

- communicating more clearly and confidently
- maintaining consistency across different environments
- ensuring your actions reflect your beliefs
- presenting yourself with greater intentionality

Small adjustments in consistency create a strong and authentic presence over time.

When your identity is clear, your brand becomes a natural extension of who you are, not something you need to construct, but something you consistently reflect.

A Dua to Carry With You

Dua for good character

اللَّهُمَّ اهْدِنِي لِأَحْسَنِ الأَخْلَاقِ، لَا يَهْدِي لِأَحْسَنِهَا إِلَّا أَنْتَ، وَاصْرِفْ عَنِّي سَيِّئَهَا، لَا يَصْرِفُ عَنِّي سَيِّئَهَا إِلَّا أَنْتَ

Transliteration:

Allāhumma ihdinī li-aḥsani al-akhlāq, lā yahdī li-aḥsani-hā illā anta, waṣrif ʿannī sayyiʾahā, lā yaṣrifu ʿannī sayyiʾahā illā anta.

Translation:

O Allah, guide me to the best of character, for none guides to the best of it except You; and turn away from me bad character, for none turns it away except You. (Muslim)

This supplication reminds us that true beauty lies in character.

PURE Practice

One Simple Micro-Practice

At the end of each day, ask yourself:

Did my actions today reflect the values I want to be known for?

This simple reflection strengthens awareness and alignment over time.

CHAPTER TEN

Influence: Using Your Voice With Clarity and Responsibility

Principle Introduction

Influence is often misunderstood.

It is commonly associated with visibility, platforms or positions of authority. Many assume that influence belongs to those who are widely recognised, followed or heard on a large scale, but influence begins long before any of that. It exists in everyday interactions.

It exists in the way a person speaks, in the way they respond to challenges, in the standards they uphold.

Every time someone observes your behaviour, listens to your words or is affected by your presence, influence is taking place.

Whether intentional or not.

As a Muslim woman building a life of faith, wealth and legacy, influence is not something to avoid, it is something to become conscious of because once influence is recognised, it becomes a responsibility.

Words carry weight. They can guide, uplift and clarify or they can confuse, discourage and mislead.

Silence, too, carries weight.

There are moments where choosing not to speak allows what is wrong to continue unchallenged and there are moments where restraint reflects wisdom.

Learning to navigate this balance requires awareness, intention and sincerity.

Within the PURE Framework, influence is not about being the loudest voice in the room, it is about being a clear and principled one.

The PURE Connection

The Leader

Amirah had recently been asked to coordinate a small group of sisters within her local community circle.

It wasn't something she had actively sought, but over time, her consistency, reliability and quiet presence had made her someone others naturally turned to.

At first, she approached it simply, organising sessions, ensuring things ran smoothly, keeping everything on track.

But gradually, she began to notice something shift.

Her words carried weight.

When she spoke, others listened more attentively. When she suggested something, it was followed. Even her reactions, moments of approval, hesitation or concern influenced the tone of the group.

One evening, during a planning discussion for a community initiative, a decision needed to be made.

The easier option was clear. It would keep things simple and avoid delay. But it also overlooked a concern one of the sisters had mentioned, quietly and almost in passing.

Amirah paused.

She sensed the group waiting.

In that moment, she became aware of something deeper. Her response would not only shape the decision, it would shape the environment. She could move quickly and keep things easy or she could create space, even if it required more time.

She chose to pause the discussion and return to the concern. The conversation became longer, more layered and less convenient.

But something shifted.

The sisters began to speak more openly, they felt heard, they contributed with more confidence. The space changed.

In that moment, she realised leadership was not about position, it was about presence. About the ability to shape a space through intention, awareness and responsibility and from that point on, she no longer approached her role as simply organising.

She approached it as guiding.

Firdaws Reflection

Influence begins with awareness.

Reflect on the following:

- In which areas of your life do people look to you for guidance or direction?
- How do your words and actions affect those around you?
- Are there moments when you hold back from speaking with clarity?
- How intentional are you about the impact you have on others?

Influence is not something you step into later.

It is something you are already exercising.

Wisdom Unfolded

The Prophet ﷺ said:

"He who believes in Allah and the Last Day must either speak good or remain silent."
(Bukhari & Muslim)

This hadith establishes a powerful principle. It teaches that speech is not neutral.

It carries consequences. A believer is therefore encouraged to speak when there is benefit, and to remain silent when words may cause harm or hold no value.

This balance forms the foundation of responsible influence.

It is not about speaking often. It is about speaking with purpose.

Principle in Action

Strengthening Your Influence

Influence becomes meaningful when it is exercised with clarity and intention.

Use the following exercise to become more aware of how you use your voice.

Step One — Recognise Where You Already Influence

Consider the spaces where your presence has an impact:

- your workplace or professional environment
- your family or close relationships
- your community or social circles

Ask yourself:
Where do my words and actions shape the thinking or behaviour of others?

Step Two — Evaluate Your Communication

Reflect on how you currently express yourself.

- Do you communicate clearly and confidently?
- Do you hold back when clarity is needed?
- Are your words aligned with your values?

Ask yourself:

Does my communication reflect the standards I want to uphold?

Step Three — Practice Intentional Expression

Choose one area where you can strengthen your influence.

This may include:

- speaking with greater clarity in discussions
- addressing concerns rather than avoiding them
- offering guidance when it is needed
- using your voice to uplift and support others

Influence grows when expression becomes intentional.

When your voice is guided by clarity and sincerity, it becomes a means of positive impact.

A Dua to Carry With You

Dua for truthfulness in speech and action

اللَّهُمَّ إِنِّي أَسْأَلُكَ الصِّدْقَ فِي الْقَوْلِ وَالْعَمَلِ

Transliteration:

Allāhumma innī asʾaluka aṣ-ṣidqa fī al-qawli wa-l-ʿamal

Translation:

O Allah, I ask You for truthfulness in speech and action. *(Ahmad)*

Return to this supplication, especially in those moments when you feel the pull to compromise your honesty. It helps you remain sincere, sharpens your integrity and keeps you accountable to a higher standard.

PURE Practice

One Simple Micro-Practice

Before speaking in an important moment, pause briefly and ask yourself:

Will my words bring clarity, benefit or guidance?

This small pause strengthens awareness and helps align your influence with intention.

CHAPTER ELEVEN

Integrity: Aligning Your Actions With Your Beliefs

Principle Introduction

Integrity is the foundation upon which trust is built.

It is not defined by what a person says, but by what they consistently do.

In moments of ease, integrity is rarely tested. It is in moments of pressure, when compromise is easier, when no one is watching, when the outcome feels uncertain, that integrity becomes visible.

A person may speak with clarity, they may present themselves with confidence, they may be recognised for their influence, but without integrity, these qualities lose their weight because over time, inconsistency becomes apparent.

Within the PURE Framework, integrity is not an external performance, it is an internal alignment. It is the ability to ensure that your actions reflect your values, even when doing so requires restraint, patience or sacrifice. Integrity is deeply connected to consciousness of Allah ﷻ. It is the awareness that even when actions go unseen by others, they remain known to Him.

This awareness creates a quiet form of accountability, one that does not depend on recognition but on sincerity.

Integrity, therefore, becomes a stabilising force, it ensures that growth remains grounded, that influence remains trustworthy and that success does not come at the cost of alignment.

The PURE Connection

The Leader

Khadijah had built a strong reputation within her field.

She was known for her professionalism, her attention to detail and her ability to deliver results under pressure. Over time, this consistency had earned her both respect and opportunity.

One particular opportunity, however, presented a different kind of challenge.

She was invited to be part of a project that carried significant visibility and potential for advancement. It was the kind of opportunity that could accelerate her career and position her within influential circles. At first glance, it seemed like a natural step forward, but as she became more familiar with the details, she noticed certain aspects that did not sit comfortably with her. There were expectations within the project that blurred lines she had always been careful to maintain. Nothing overtly wrong, but subtle compromises, the kind that are often overlooked in pursuit of progress.

She found herself at a crossroads.

One path offered advancement, recognition and immediate benefit. The other required her to step back, potentially missing an opportunity she had worked hard to reach.

The decision was not simple.

She understood the value of growth. She recognised the effort she had invested to reach this stage, but she also understood the importance of remaining aligned.

After careful reflection, she made her decision. She chose to step back. It was not a decision she announced publicly, nor was it one that others fully understood, but it was one she made with clarity.

In the days that followed, she felt a quiet sense of steadiness. The opportunity had passed, but her alignment remained intact and over time, that consistency continued to shape how she was trusted, respected and relied upon.

Firdaws Reflection

Integrity invites you to examine alignment.

Reflect on the following:

- Are your actions consistently aligned with your values?
- Have you faced situations where compromise felt easier than standing firm?
- What influences your decisions in moments of pressure?
- How do you define integrity within your own life?

Integrity is not something that can be formed in a single moment, but something that is built through repeated choices.

Wisdom Unfolded

Allah ﷻ says:

"O you who have believed, fear Allah and be with those who are true."
(Qur'an 9:119)

Truthfulness is not limited to speech; it extends to actions, intentions and consistency. To be among those who are truthful is to live in a way where what is seen reflects what is real.

The Prophet ﷺ was known as Al-Ameen, the trustworthy. His character was recognised even before his prophethood. This reflects the weight of integrity.

It is something that becomes evident over time, through consistent alignment between belief and action.

Principle in Action

Strengthening Your Integrity

Integrity is strengthened through awareness and intentional choice.

Use the following exercise to examine and reinforce alignment in your life.

Step One — Identify Areas of Potential Misalignment

Reflect on situations where your actions may not fully reflect your values.

This could include:

- decisions made under pressure
- moments where you remained silent when clarity was needed

- situations where convenience or cultural pressures influenced your choices

Ask yourself:

Where might I be compromising without fully acknowledging it?

Step Two — Clarify Your Non-Negotiables

Define the principles you are not willing to compromise.

These may relate to:

- honesty and transparency
- ethical decision-making
- professional conduct
- personal boundaries

Ask yourself:

What standards do I want to uphold, regardless of circumstance?

Step Three — Prepare for Future Decisions

Integrity is easier to maintain when decisions are made in advance.

Consider:

- how you would respond if faced with a similar situation again
- what boundaries you would reinforce

- what outcomes you are willing to accept in order to remain aligned

Clarity reduces hesitation when moments of decision arise.

Integrity is not always the easiest path, but it is the one that creates stability, trust and long-term respect.

A Dua to Carry With You

Dua for trust and reliance on Allah ﷻ

رَبَّنَآ إِنَّكَ تَعۡلَمُ مَا نُخۡفِي وَمَا نُعۡلِنُۗ وَمَا يَخۡفَىٰ عَلَى ٱللَّهِ مِن شَيۡءٖ فِي ٱلۡأَرۡضِ وَلَا فِي ٱلسَّمَآءِ

Transliteration:

Rabbanaaa innaka ta'lamu maa nukhfee wa maa nu'lin; wa maa yakhfaa 'alal laahi min shai'in fil ardi wa laa fis samaaa'

Translation:

Our Lord, indeed You know what we conceal and what we declare, and nothing is hidden from Allah on the earth or in the heavens. (Muslim)

This supplication is a reminder that Allah ﷻ knows the intent behind our actions, whether they be sincere or disingenuous.

PURE Practice

One Simple Micro-Practice

In a moment of decision this week, pause and ask yourself:

Does this choice reflect who I want to be before Allah ﷻ?

This brief pause can redirect actions toward alignment.

CHAPTER TWELVE

Authority: Building Trust Through Consistency and Credibility

Principle Introduction

Authority is often misunderstood as position.

It is associated with titles, recognition or visible leadership roles. Many assume that authority is granted externally, through promotion, status or public acknowledgement, but within the PURE Framework, authority is not given.

It is **built**.

It develops over time, through consistency in character, clarity in communication and reliability in action. It is the natural outcome of a life where values are expressed and also upheld repeatedly.

Authority is what remains when words, actions and intentions align, it is reflected in how a person is trusted, in how their presence is received, in how others turn to them. Not because they are required to, but because they recognise a level of steadiness and credibility.

For a Muslim woman building a life of faith, wealth and legacy, authority is not about control, it is about responsibility.

It is the position of being someone others rely on for clarity, direction or example and with that comes a deeper level of accountability.

Because authority amplifies impact, what you say carries further, what you do influences more and what you represent becomes more visible.

Authority, when rooted in sincerity, becomes a means of service.

It allows a person to guide, support and influence in ways that extend beyond themselves.

The PURE Connection

The Authority

Sumayyah had spent years building her work quietly.

She was consistent, thoughtful and committed to maintaining a high standard in everything she did. She did not seek attention, nor did she position herself as a leader. She simply focused on doing her work well.

Over time, something began to shift. People started coming to her for guidance. At first, it was occasional, a colleague asking for advice, a peer seeking her perspective on a decision, but gradually, it became more frequent. Her input was sought in discussions, her opinion was valued in decision-making, her presence began to carry weight.

It was not simply that people trusted her, they trusted her judgement. They had seen her approach situations with thought and care, they had seen her make decisions that were measured, considered and effective. Over time, a pattern had formed, when she spoke, it was not based on impulse, it was based on consistency.

One particular moment made this clear.

During a complex project, a disagreement arose within the team. There were multiple perspectives, each strongly held, and the discussion had reached a point of tension. After some time, someone turned to her and said:

"What do you think we should do?"

The room quieted. This was not because she held a formal position of authority, it was because her judgement had proven itself over time. People were not simply listening, they were relying on her ability to see clearly and decide well.

In that moment, she recognised something important. Authority had not been something she pursued, it had been something she built through her actions, through her consistency, through her ability to make decisions that others could trust and now, it carried responsibility.

Firdaws Reflection

Authority is reflected in how you are trusted.

Reflect on the following:

- In which areas of your life do others rely on your judgement?
- What patterns of behaviour have contributed to that trust?
- Are there areas where you would like to strengthen your credibility?
- How do you carry responsibility when others look to you for guidance?

Authority is not defined by position; it is defined by consistency.

Wisdom Unfolded

Allah ﷻ says:

“Indeed, the best one you can hire is the strong and the trustworthy.”

(Qur’an 28:26)

This verse highlights two essential qualities:

Strength (capability) and trustworthiness (integrity).

Authority is formed at the intersection of these qualities.

A person may be capable, but without trust, their influence is limited.

A person may be trustworthy, but without capability, their impact may not reach its full potential. When both are present, authority becomes established.

Principle in Action

Building Your Authority

Authority is developed intentionally through consistent behaviour over time.

Use the following exercise to strengthen your credibility and presence.

Step One — Identify Your Area of Strength

Reflect on where your capability lies.

- What are you known for?
- Where do you consistently deliver value?
- In which areas do others seek your input?

Clarity in your strengths allows you to build authority with focus.

Step Two — Strengthen Your Reliability

Authority grows through consistency.

Ask yourself:

- Do I follow through on commitments?
- Do I maintain the same standards across different situations?
- Can others depend on my word and actions?

Reliability builds trust over time.

Step Three — Carry Responsibility With Intention

When others begin to rely on you, your actions extend beyond yourself.

Consider:

- how your decisions affect those around you
- how your example influences others
- how you can use your position to guide with sincerity

Authority is not simply about being trusted, it is about honouring that trust and authority is not built in a single moment, it is established through consistent alignment over time.

A Dua to Carry With You

Dua for trustworthy leadership and service

اللَّهُمَّ اجعلني هادياً للناس بالخير، وموفِّقاً لما تحب وترضى

Transliteration:

Allāhumma ajʿalnī hādiyan li-n-nāsi bil-khayr, wa muwaffiqan limā tuḥibbu wa tarda

Translation:

O Allah, make me a guide to people in goodness and grant me success in that which You love and are pleased with.

(Muslim & Ahmad)

This supplication reflects the desire to be a guiding role model who leads others in goodness and what pleases Allah ﷻ.

PURE Practice

One Simple Micro-Practice

Choose one commitment this week and fulfil it with complete excellence and consistency.

Authority is strengthened in small, consistent actions.

PART FOUR

Emaan

Spiritual Depth That Anchors Everything

ٱلَّذِينَ ءَامَنُواْ وَتَطْمَئِنُّ قُلُوبُهُم بِذِكْرِ ٱللَّهِۗ أَلَا بِذِكْرِ ٱللَّهِ تَطْمَئِنُّ ٱلْقُلُوبُ ٢٨

'Those who have believed and whose hearts are assured by the remembrance of Allah. Unquestionably, by the remembrance of Allah, hearts are assured.'

Surah Al-Ra'd 13:28

The heart finds its true stability not in worldly success, but in remembrance of the One who grants it.

PURE INTRODUCTION

EMAAN

Spiritual Depth That Anchors Worldly Expansion

As a woman builds her life, her wealth, her relationships and her influence, her world begins to expand.

With that expansion comes opportunity, but it also brings something less visible.

Pressure.

Expectation.

Attachment.

What once felt intentional can begin to feel demanding. What once felt aligned can slowly become driven by outcome rather than sincerity.

This is where Emaan becomes essential, Emaan is what protects growth, it is the inner state that ensures that as a woman rises in her external life, she does not lose her internal grounding. It safeguards her heart from becoming overly attached to what she is building, reminding her that everything she has is temporary and entrusted to her by Allah ﷻ.

Emaan also sustains more than worship alone; it anchors sleep, recovery and the inner steadiness required when responsibilities across every area of life grow heavier at once.

Without Emaan, growth can become unbalanced, success may be achieved, but at the cost of peace, recognition may increase, but sincerity may weaken, wealth may grow, but the heart may become attached to it.

With Emaan, everything returns to alignment, it brings intention back into focus, it restores sincerity in action, it creates a sense of calm within expansion.

Emaan is built through consistency, through the small, often unseen actions that maintain a connection with Allah ﷻ, through prayer performed with presence, through remembrance carried throughout the day, through returning to Allah ﷻ in moments of both ease and difficulty.

Within the PURE Framework, Emaan is expressed through four principles:

Refinement — Continually purifying the heart, intentions and actions

Consistency — Honouring the small deeds that sustain spiritual strength

Reliance — Working with excellence while trusting Allah ﷻ with outcomes

Balance — Pursuing dunya without neglecting the akhirah

Together, these principles ensure that growth does not lead to disconnection, but to deeper alignment.

Because the ultimate goal is not only what you build in this world, it is who you become before Allah ﷻ.

CHAPTER THIRTEEN

Refinement: Continually Purifying the Heart, Intentions and Actions

Principle Introduction

Not all growth is visible.

A person may build a life that appears complete, structured, successful and impactful. Yet beneath what is seen, there remains an inner world that requires continuous attention.

The state of the heart.

Refinement is the process of returning to that inner space, it is the ongoing effort to purify intentions, to realign actions and to ensure that what is done outwardly remains sincere inwardly.

Actions alone are not what define a believer, it is the intention behind them.

A person may achieve success, contribute to others and be recognised for their efforts, but without refinement, subtle shifts can occur. Intentions may become mixed, actions may become routine rather than conscious, the heart may begin to seek what is seen, rather than what is accepted.

Refinement brings awareness back, it allows a woman to pause and ask:

Why am I doing what I am doing?

Who is this truly for?

For a Muslim woman building a life of faith, wealth and legacy, refinement ensures that growth remains anchored in sincerity.

It protects the heart from becoming attached to recognition, it redirects focus toward acceptance by Allah ﷻ and it reminds her that what is unseen often carries more weight than what is visible.

The PURE Connection

The Reflective One

Safiyyah had built a life she once prayed for.

Her work was meaningful, her responsibilities were expanding, she was contributing in ways that brought benefit to others, and she was recognised for her efforts.

From the outside, everything appeared aligned and for a long time, she felt a sense of fulfilment in what she was building, but gradually, something within her began to feel different. It was not a clear shift, more of a subtle awareness. Moments where she noticed her thoughts lingering on how her work was perceived. A quiet anticipation of recognition after completing something significant. A sense of disappointment when her efforts went unnoticed.

At first, she dismissed it, these were small thoughts, natural, perhaps. But over time, they became more noticeable. Until one evening, after completing a project she had invested deeply in, she paused. She had done everything well, yet instead of feeling content, her mind drifted toward whether it would be acknowledged.

That moment unsettled her; she realised her intention was not sincere. Later that night, she sat in reflection, she asked herself a question she had not considered in some time:

If no one saw this, would it still hold the same value to me?

The question stayed with her. It was uncomfortable, but it was necessary.

In the days that followed, she began to return to small acts of intention-setting. Before beginning her work, she paused. She reminded herself of who she was doing it for.

Nothing external changed, but internally, something began to shift.

Her actions felt lighter, more grounded because they were no longer tied to what was seen, they were anchored in something deeper.

Firdaws Reflection

Refinement begins with honest awareness.

Reflect on the following:

- What motivates your actions most consistently?
- Do you find yourself seeking recognition or validation?
- How often do you pause to check your intention?
- If certain actions were unseen, would they still hold the same value to you?

Refinement is about returning again and again to sincerity.

Wisdom Unfolded

The Prophet ﷺ said:
"Actions are judged by intentions, and every person will have what they intended."
(Bukhari & Muslim)

This hadith establishes one of the most foundational principles in Islam.

It reminds us that the value of an action is not only in what is done, but in the intention behind it.

Two people may perform the same action.

But their outcomes may differ completely based on what resides in their hearts.

Refinement, therefore, is the continuous effort to purify that intention.

Principle in Action

The Sincerity Reset

Refinement is a practice of awareness and return.

Use the following exercise to strengthen sincerity while identifying, confronting and retraining insincere intentions.

Step One — Identify Where You Are Seen

Write down 2–3 areas where your actions are most visible.

This may include:

- acts of worship

- your work or achievements
- helping or leading others

Then ask yourself:

Where do I feel the need to be recognised?

Be honest.

Step Two — Pause the Intention

Before your next visible action, pause and ask:

"If no one knew I did this... would I still do it in the same way?"

Do not move forward until you answer sincerely.

Let it challenge you.

Step Three — The Hidden Action

Choose **one action** to do consistently, unseen.

Something only Allah ﷻ knows.

Do it quietly.

Without mention.

Without a hint.

Commit to this.

Step Four — Withdraw the Audience

Choose one area where you usually share or seek visibility.

Then intentionally reduce it, delay it or remove it entirely.

Observe:

Does your motivation remain or change?

Sincerity is strengthened when the need to be seen is removed.

A Dua to Carry With You

Dua for a life of Ihsan and steadfast guidance

رَبَّنَا لَا تُزِغْ قُلُوبَنَا بَعْدَ إِذْ هَدَيْتَنَا وَهَبْ لَنَا مِن لَّدُنكَ رَحْمَةً ۚ إِنَّكَ أَنتَ الْوَهَّابُ

Transliteration:

Rabbana lā tuzigh qulūbanā baʿda idh hadaytanā wa hab lanā min ladunka raḥmah, innaka anta al-Wahhāb

Translation:

Our Lord, do not let our hearts deviate after You have guided us, and grant us mercy from Yourself. Indeed, You are the Bestower. *(Al-Qur'an 3:8)*

This supplication reflects the believer's awareness that sincerity requires constant protection.

PURE Practice

One Simple Micro-Practice

Before one task each day, pause and consciously renew your intention for the sake of Allah.

Keep it simple, but keep it consistent.

CHAPTER FOURTEEN

Consistency: Honouring the Small Deeds That Sustain Spiritual Strength

Principle Introduction

Many people approach growth with intensity.

They begin with strong intention, high motivation and a desire to change quickly. For a period of time, they may increase their ibaadat, establish routines and feel deeply connected. But over time, that intensity becomes difficult to sustain.

Life becomes busy, energy shifts, responsibilities increase and gradually, what once felt strong begins to fade.

Consistency addresses this cycle.

It shifts the focus from doing more... to doing what can be sustained.

Within Islam, consistency holds immense value, it is not the scale of an action that carries the most weight, but its continuity. Small, repeated actions create a rhythm of connection that remains steady through changing circumstances.

For a Muslim sister building a life of faith, wealth and legacy, this principle is essential because her life is not static. It moves through different seasons, periods of growth, challenge, responsibility and rest.

Consistency allows her to remain connected to Allah ﷻ through all of them. It removes the pressure of perfection and replaces it with the discipline of continuity.

The PURE Connection

The Striver

Sabira had always approached her spiritual growth with sincerity.

There were periods in her life where she felt deeply connected, praying with presence, maintaining regular dhikr and engaging with the Qur'an consistently.

In those moments, everything felt aligned, but she also noticed a pattern. These periods were often followed by a gradual decline.

Her schedule would become busier. Her energy would shift. What once felt manageable would begin to feel difficult to maintain.

She would miss a practice here and there, then gradually, the routine would fall away.

Each time, she felt a quiet sense of disappointment from the struggle of sustaining what she had started.

One evening, after reflecting on this pattern, she came across a reminder:

The most beloved deeds to Allah are those that are consistent, even if they are small.

The words stayed with her.

She realised that her approach had been shaped by intensity rather than sustainability. She had been trying to do more but not necessarily to do what she could maintain.

The shift was simple but significant.

Instead of building large routines, she began to focus on smaller, consistent actions, a short portion of the Qur'an each day, a moment of dhikr after prayer, a simple dua she returned to regularly. Nothing felt overwhelming; it felt steady.

Over time, something changed, her connection no longer came in waves, it became continuous and within that consistency, she found something she had not experienced before.

Stability.

Firdaws Reflection

Consistency begins with honesty.

Reflect on the following:

- Do you tend to approach spiritual growth in cycles of intensity?
- Which practices have you struggled to maintain consistently?
- What feels sustainable within your current season of life?
- Are you placing pressure on yourself to do more than you can sustain?

Consistency is not about doing everything.

It is about doing something… consistently.

Wisdom Unfolded

The Prophet ﷺ said:

"The most beloved deeds to Allah ﷻ are those done consistently, even if they are few."
(Al-Bukhari & Muslim)

This hadith provides a clear framework for sustainable growth.

It removes the emphasis on scale and places it on continuity.

A small action, when repeated consistently, becomes more beloved than a large action performed occasionally.

This principle transforms how a believer approaches ibaadat.

It shifts the goal from intensity to steadiness.

Principle in Action

Building Sustainable Consistency

Consistency is built through simplicity and intention.

Use the following exercise to establish practices that you can maintain.

Step One — Start Smaller Than You Think

Choose one or two actions that feel manageable within your current routine.

This could include:

- reading a small portion of the Qur'an daily
- making dhikr after one prayer

- setting aside a few minutes for dua

Ask yourself:

Can I sustain this on my busiest days?

If the answer is yes, you are starting at the right level.

Step Two — Anchor Actions to Existing Habits

Consistency becomes easier when actions are linked to something already established.

For example:

- dhikr after salah
- dua before sleeping
- reflection during a quiet moment in the day

Anchoring reduces the effort required to remember.

Step Three — Protect Continuity, Not Perfection

There will be days when energy is low.

On those days, reduce the action, but do not remove it.

Even a minimal version maintains the habit.

Consistency is built by continuing, not by stopping.

Over time, these small actions create a lasting connection.

A Dua to Carry With You

Dua for consistency and steadfastness

رَبَّنَا أَفْرِغْ عَلَيْنَا صَبْرًا وَثَبِّتْ أَقْدَامَنَا

Transliteration:

Rabbana afrigh ʿalaynā ṣabran wa thabbit aqdāmanā

Translation:

Our Lord, pour upon us patience and make our steps firm.

(Al-Qur'an 2:250)

This supplication reflects the need for Allah's ﷻ support in maintaining consistency.

PURE Practice

One Simple Micro-Practice

Choose one small act of worship and commit to it daily for the next 7 days.

Keep it simple.

Keep it consistent.

CHAPTER FIFTEEN

Reliance: Working With Excellence While Trusting Allah With Outcomes

Principle Introduction

As women, we often feel a desire to control outcomes, to plan carefully, to make the right decisions and ensure that the effort leads to the results we hope for.

This desire is not wrong.

In fact, striving for excellence is encouraged. A believer is taught to act with intention, to prepare and to put in effort with sincerity.

But alongside effort, there is something equally important.

Tawakkul. Reliance on Allah ﷻ.

Tawakkul is often misunderstood as passivity, as if trusting Allah ﷻ means stepping back or doing less, true reliance is not the absence of effort, it is the balance between effort and surrender.

It is doing what is within your control, while accepting that outcomes are not.

For a Muslim woman building a life of faith, wealth and legacy, this principle becomes essential because as her responsibilities grow, so do the variables she cannot control.

Opportunities may not unfold as expected, plans may shift, results may be delayed.

Without reliance, these moments can create anxiety, frustration or doubt.

With tawakkul, perspective shifts, effort remains strong but the heart becomes lighter, no longer carrying what was never meant to be controlled.

The PURE Connection

The Planner

Imaan had always approached her life with intention.

She planned carefully, set clear goals and worked diligently toward them. Her structure gave her a sense of stability and direction.

For the most part, it served her well, but there were moments where, despite her effort, outcomes did not align with her expectations.

One particular situation stood out, she had worked toward an opportunity she deeply valued. She had prepared thoroughly, done everything within her control and approached it with sincerity. Yet the outcome did not unfold as she had hoped.

At first, she tried to understand what had gone wrong.

Had she missed something?

Could she have done more?

She revisited every detail, searching for an explanation that would make the result feel justified but gradually, she realised something.

She had done what she could, the rest had never been in her control.

That realisation was not immediate in bringing ease, but it opened the door to a different way of thinking. Instead of measuring her effort by outcome, she began to measure it by sincerity and excellence.

Instead of holding tightly to what she wanted, she began to trust that what unfolded carried wisdom she could not yet see.

Over time, this shift changed her experience of effort. She continued to plan, she continued to strive, but she no longer carried the same weight of expectation. She understood that her role was to act and Allah's role was to determine what followed.

Firdaws Reflection

Reliance begins where control ends.

Reflect on the following:

- In which areas of your life do you feel the strongest need to control outcomes?
- How do you respond when things do not go as planned?
- Do you measure your effort by results or by sincerity?
- What would it feel like to trust Allah ﷻ more deeply with your outcomes?

Tawakkul is not the absence of planning; it is the presence of trust.

Wisdom Unfolded

Allah ﷻ says:

"And whoever relies upon Allah – then He is sufficient for him." *(Qur'an 65:3)*

This verse offers a powerful reassurance.

It reminds the believer that reliance on Allah ﷻ is not empty.

It is supported.

When a person places their trust in Allah ﷻ, they are not left alone with their circumstances. They are held within a greater wisdom that extends beyond what they can see.

Tawakkul, therefore, brings both strength and ease.

Principle in Action

Strengthening Your Tawakkul

Reliance is developed through conscious shifts in how you approach effort and outcome.

Use the following exercise to strengthen this balance.

Step One — Define What Is Within Your Control

Identify the aspects of your situation that you can influence.

This may include:

- your effort
- your preparation
- your intentions
- your decisions

Focus your energy here.

Step Two — Release What Is Beyond Your Control

Now recognise what you cannot control.

- timing
- outcomes
- other people's responses
- external circumstances

Ask yourself:
Am I holding onto something that was never mine to carry?

Step Three — Pair Effort With Trust

As you take action, consciously connect it with reliance.

- make dua before and after the effort
- remind yourself that results are in Allah's ﷻ hands
- accept outcomes with trust, even when they differ from expectations

Tawakkul is strengthened through repetition.

When reliance is present, effort becomes lighter, and outcomes are received with greater peace.

A Dua to Carry With You

Dua for reliance upon Allah

حَسْبِيَ اللَّهُ لَا إِلَٰهَ إِلَّا هُوَ ۖ عَلَيْهِ تَوَكَّلْتُ ۖ وَهُوَ رَبُّ الْعَرْشِ الْعَظِيمِ

Transliteration:

Hasbiyal laahu laaa ilaaha illaa Huwa 'alaihi tawakkkaltu wa Huwa Rabbul 'Arshil 'Azeem

Translation:

Sufficient for me is Allah; there is no deity except Him. On Him I have relied, and He is the Lord of the Great Throne.

(Qur'an 9:129)

This supplication anchors the heart in trust.

PURE Practice

One Simple Micro-Practice

When faced with a decision this week, especially one you feel uncertain about, turn to Salat al-Istikhara.

This prayer is **not only** for major life decisions like marriage.

It is for any moment where you are unsure how to move forward.

Pray two rakah.

Make the dua of istikhara with presence.

If you are unfamiliar with it, you can find it in trusted sources such as *Fortress of the Muslim* or through reliable dua apps.

Then proceed with what feels clear, trusting that Allah ﷻ will guide what is best.

Do your part with sincerity and trust Allah ﷻ with what unfolds.

CHAPTER SIXTEEN

Balance: Pursuing Dunya Without Neglecting the Akhirah

Principle Introduction

A life of faith is not meant to be divided.

It is not a choice between dunya and akhirah, nor is it a constant tension between ambition and spirituality, it is a balance.

A Muslim woman is not asked to withdraw from the world in order to preserve her faith, she is asked to move through it with awareness. to build, while remembering, to strive, while remaining grounded, to pursue, while staying aligned.

Balance is not about equal distribution; it is about correct prioritisation. It is the ability to place each aspect of life in its rightful position, ensuring that what is temporary does not overshadow what is eternal.

Without balance, life can become fragmented, a person may become consumed by their goals, losing sight of their spiritual grounding or they may withdraw from growth, fearing that ambition will distance them from their faith.

But when balance is present, both can exist in harmony, worldly effort becomes an extension of intention and spiritual connection remains constant, regardless of external growth.

The PURE Connection

The Integrator

Aadila had spent years trying to find balance.

At different stages of her life, she found herself leaning in different directions. There were times when her focus was heavily on growth, building her career, expanding her opportunities and striving toward goals she had set for herself. In those periods, she felt productive, but often, something felt slightly out of place.

Her spiritual practices became rushed, reflection felt limited, connection felt present, but not as deep as she desired.

At other times, she shifted in the opposite direction, she became more focused on ibaadat, creating space for reflection and prioritising her spiritual routines. In those moments, she felt grounded, but she also noticed a hesitation toward pursuing certain opportunities, as though growth and spirituality could not fully coexist.

For a long time, she moved between these two states, until one realisation changed her perspective.

She had been approaching balance as separation, as if different parts of her life needed to be placed in opposition to one another.

But what if they were not meant to compete?

What if they were meant to align?

That shift changed how she approached her life, she no longer saw her work as separate from her faith. She began to approach it with intention. Her efforts became acts of responsibility, her decisions became guided by values, her growth became connected to purpose. At the same time, she maintained her spiritual practices, not as something separate, but as something that sustained everything else.

Nothing in her life was removed, but everything became aligned and within that alignment, she found something she had been seeking for a long time.

Peace.

Firdaws Reflection

Balance begins with perspective.

Reflect on the following:

- Do you feel tension between your worldly goals and your spiritual life?
- Are there areas where one is consistently prioritised at the expense of the other?
- What would it look like to align, rather than separate, these aspects of your life?
- How can your current responsibilities become acts of intention?

Balance is not found by doing less, it is found by aligning more.

Wisdom Unfolded

Allah ﷻ says:

"But seek, through that which Allah has given you, the home of the Hereafter; and [yet], do not forget your share of the world."
(Qur'an 28:77)

This verse provides a complete framework for balance.

It encourages the believer to prioritise the akhirah, while still engaging with the dunya.

It does not call for withdrawal, it calls for alignment.

This is the essence of a balanced life.

Principle in Action

Living in Alignment

Balance is sustained through awareness and intention and by connecting what you already do to a greater purpose.

Use the following exercise to integrate your worldly and spiritual life.

Step One — Unify Your Intentions

Look at your current responsibilities:

- your work
- your family roles
- your daily commitments

Now ask:

How can each of these become an act of ibadah?

Reframe them with intention:

Providing → as amanah

Working → as a responsibility

Caring → as service for the sake of Allah ﷻ

Do not change the task.

Change the intention behind it.

Step Two — Anchor Your Day in Ibadah

Choose a few non-negotiable anchors that structure your day:

- salah at its proper time
- daily dhikr
- a moment with the Qur'an

These are not additions; they are what your day is built around.

Everything else fits around them.

Step Three — Connect to the Bigger Picture

Before committing to anything new, pause and ask:

How does this serve my akhirah?

Reflect:

- Does this draw me closer to Allah ﷻ?
- Can this be done with sincerity and integrity?
- What will this mean beyond this moment?

When your actions are connected to the Hereafter, your life stops feeling divided.

Balance is not about separating dunya and akhirah; it is about living in a way where both move in the same direction.

A Dua to Carry With You

Dua for guidance

اللَّهُمَّ اهْدِنِي وَسَدِّدْنِي

Transliteration:
Allāhumma ihdinī wa saddidnī

Translation:
O Allah, guide me and keep me upright.
(Muslim)

This supplication anchors perspective.

PURE Practice

One Simple Micro-Practice

Choose one daily activity and consciously connect it to your intention for the akhirah.

Even something small.

Let it remind you that your life is not divided.

It is directed.

CLOSING CHAPTER

The Return : A Life Built With Intention, A Return Anchored in Faith

Closing Reflection

You have now journeyed through:

- **Purpose** — defining how you live
- **Unity** — strengthening how you connect
- **Reputation** — shaping how you are seen and trusted
- **Emaan** — anchoring who you are becoming

This is the PURE Framework.

Not as a concept, but as a way of living.

A way of building a life that is:

- intentional
- aligned
- impactful
- and anchored in faith

A life that does not require you to choose between growth and spirituality, but invites you to bring them together.

The goal was never about what you build in this world, it was always about who you are becoming for in the next.

Closing

You have reached the end of this book, but in many ways, you are standing at the beginning, because this book was about recognising.

Recognising the life you are building.

Recognising the direction you are moving in.

Recognising who you are becoming, with every decision you make.

Throughout these pages, you have been invited to reflect on four dimensions of your life:

Your **Purpose** — how you live and what you build

Your **Unity** — who you connect with and grow alongside

Your **Reputation** — how you are known, trusted and experienced

Your **Emaan** — who you are before Allah ﷻ

These are dimensions that are interconnected with each other; each one strengthens the other and together, they form a way of living that is both grounded and expansive.

A life where faith is not placed to the side, but at the centre.

You may not leave this book with everything perfectly aligned, because alignment is not achieved in a single moment, it is returned to again and again.

In small decisions.

In quiet reflections.

In moments where you pause and choose differently.

There will be days when clarity feels strong, and days when it feels distant.

There will be moments where you feel deeply connected, and others where you feel stretched, distracted or uncertain.

This is part of the journey, you are allowed to build, to pursue opportunities, to grow in your work, to create, to contribute and to lead.

You are also called to remain anchored, to protect your heart, to refine your intentions, to remember that everything you hold is temporary and everything you do carries weight beyond what is seen.

This is the balance.

As you return to these principles again and again across different seasons of your life; through career shifts, family changes, moments of growth and moments of challenge; you will notice something subtle taking place.

The principles stop feeling like sixteen separate practices and begin to feel like one way of living.

Your prayer begins to shape your work.

Your relationships begin to strengthen your wellbeing.

Your wealth begins to support your worship.

Your character begins to influence every space you enter.

This integration is not something you achieve once. It deepens gradually as intention stays consistent across every dimension of your life.

This is the path.

The PURE Framework is not meant to be a set of ideas you understand once and move on from.

It is something you live, it evolves with you, it meets you in different seasons and it continues to guide you as your life expands.

So as you move forward, carry this with you:

Be intentional in what you pursue.

Be grounded in who you walk alongside.

Be consistent in how you show up.

Be sincere in who you are before Allah ﷻ.

And above all, remember this:

You are not building for this world alone, you are building for what comes after it.

Every intention you set.

Every action you take.

Every choice you make.

It all contributes to a life that extends beyond what you can see.

A life that, with Allah's permission, leads to something greater.

A Final Dua

Dua for good

رَبَّنَآ ءَاتِنَا فِى ٱلدُّنْيَا حَسَنَةً وَفِى ٱلْـَٔاخِرَةِ حَسَنَةً وَقِنَا عَذَابَ ٱلنَّارِ

Transliteration:

Rabbanaa 'aatinaa fid-dunyaa hasanatan wa fil-'aakhirati hasanatan wa qinaa 'athaaban-naar.

Translation:

Our Lord! Give us in this world that which is good and in the Hereafter that which is good and save us from the torment of the Fire! *(Al-Qur'an 2:201)*

EPILOGUE

What Remains

One day, what you have built will no longer be in your hands.

The work.

The roles.

The responsibilities you carried.

All of it will be left behind.

What will remain is what was for Allah ﷻ.

The intention behind your effort.

The sincerity within your actions.

The moments you chose alignment over ease.

Nothing you did for His sake is lost.

Not the quiet discipline.

Not the unseen restraint.

Not the return after you fell short.

This life was never the destination.

It was the place you were given to build.

And now, you know how to build differently.

With intention.

With structure.

With awareness of what carries forward.

So move forward with clarity.

Apply what you have learned.

Refine as you go.

Return often.

Build a life that serves you here,

and remains for you there.

What you build matters. But what remains matters more.

ABOUT THE AUTHOR

Folu Umm Abdullah is the creator of the PURE Framework and the founder of The Firdaws Connection.

Her work is rooted in a simple reality:

Muslim women are capable of building wealth, leadership and legacy, without compromising their values.

She created The Firdaws Connection to provide what was missing:

A structured, faith-aligned approach to growth.

More than a platform for inspiration, it is a space for intentional advancement, where women are supported to build with clarity, discipline and direction.

Her work brings together faith, structure and long-term thinking, equipping women to build lives that are not only successful, but aligned.

Her conviction is simple:

When a woman builds with intention, she does not rise alone.

Her impact extends into her family, her community and her legacy.

ABOUT THE FIRDAWS CONNECTION

The Firdaws Connection was built on a simple conviction: Muslim women deserve a clear pathway from where they are now to where they are building toward; one rooted in faith, structured in practice and supported by sisters walking the same road.

What began as ideas inside these pages has grown into something you can step into directly.

Your Entry Point: The Muslim Women's Wealth Blueprint

Your first step into The Firdaws Connection is a free three-day experience called **The Muslim Women's Wealth Blueprint**.

Across three days you will work through a focused framework designed to help you:

- Clarify what you are building toward in your journey
- Identify where your current approach may be holding you back
- Establish the foundational shifts that move you from intention into action

The Blueprint is delivered live online and is completely free to attend.

It is designed for sisters who are ready to stop consuming content about wealth and start building it; with structure, with clarity and with faith at the centre.

Where It Leads: The Firdaws Network

The Muslim Women's Wealth Blueprint opens the door to **The Firdaws Network**; a private community for Muslim women committed to building wealth, leadership and legacy without compromising their values.

Inside the Network you will find:

- **Halaqas** organised by progression level; small circles where sisters build together through discussion, accountability and shared practice
- **Huda**, your weekly leadership mentor who guides your focus across every area of life being built
- **Sakina**, your reflection companion who supports your spiritual grounding through daily prompts and quiet check-ins
- **Amina**, your baseline trustee who provides structured financial tracking and weekly accountability conversations

- **Live sessions, seminars and member-led conversations** that deepen knowledge and expand what you are capable of building

The Network is not another content library or passive membership. It is an active environment where what you learn becomes what you build; alongside sisters who understand both the ambition and the amanah behind it.

What Comes After: In-Person Experiences

Alongside the digital Network, The Firdaws Connection hosts **in-person gatherings, workshops and networking events** for sisters ready to connect beyond screens.

These experiences create space for:

- Meeting sisters you have built alongside online in real life
- Workshops that go deeper than what fits inside a webinar format
- Networking opportunities that lead to collaboration, partnership and shared ventures
- Retreats designed for reflection, planning and renewal away from daily demands

Dates and locations are announced inside the Network as they are confirmed.

Our Approach

We build through progression:

Clarity → Structure → Discipline → Wealth → Legacy

Everything is designed to move you forward with intention.

A Different Standard

The Firdaws Connection is not for those looking for shortcuts.

It is for sisters ready to:

- Take responsibility for what they build
- Move with clarity and intention
- Commit to a higher standard of growth

Because what is built with structure does not only benefit the present; it carries forward.

Continue Your Journey

This book is your starting point; the next step is implementation.

If you are ready to build with clarity, structure and direction:

Visit: **www.thefirdawsconnection.com**

Build wealth with intention.

Grow with structure.

Leave what remains.

www.ingramcontent.com/pod-product-compliance
Lightning Source LLC
LaVergne TN
LVHW052322200926
848481LV00002B/638
9798904178895